For the Love
of *Arlo*

For the Love of *Arlo*

A Courageous Pup Born Different

CHRISTINA ENGLAND BA Hons

In Loving Memory of my dear friend and avid fundraiser,
Mrs. Ailsa Bowman, who sadly passed away in 2021

and

My wonderful son, Daniel England,
who sadly lost his fight for life in 2023.

Contents

Introduction

This is the true story behind my decision to foster, and eventually adopt, a six month old puppy who had been cruelly abandoned by a railway line in Romania. The reason this sweet little pup had been left to die soon became apparent when Stefan, a kind and compassionate man who owned a small rescue in the area, picked up the pup and took him back to his rescue.

Arlo, as I later named him, had been born with severe deformities in both of his front legs. The only way he could move at all was to shuffle around in the dirt on his forearms.

However, all this was about to change.

Read Arlo's remarkable story and learn how this once severely crippled and unloved pup, would one day walk tall and be surrounded by the love of a new family in the UK.

CHAPTER 1

Some Things are Just Meant to be

I have always believed that some things are just meant to be. At the time that I found out about Arlo, I already had five dogs and I certainly wasn't actively searching for a sixth one, not consciously at least!

In 2019, two dogs were rescued by *Hessa's Homeless Hounds* [1], a rescue that I had previously adopted from. Both dogs had sustained nasty injuries which were said to have been caused by an abusive owner.

One of them was adopted by a friend of mine and the other one, a Tibetan spaniel who had suffered a broken back, remained at the rescue centre to receive veterinary care and therapy before being offered up for adoption.

However, no matter how hard I tried, I kept thinking about this little dog who the rescue had named Minnie due to her size. Sadly, Minnie never found an adoptive home and in March, 2020, I decided to ask Hessa if she would consider letting me adopt her.

Hessa had always known that I wanted to adopt a disabled dog, however, when I asked about Minnie and asked her if she would allow me to adopt her, there was a long pause at the end of the phone, before Hessa said, *"I will consider it, yes, but not before I tell you about another little dog that I was contacted about yesterday."*

She continued, explaining that a rescue that she was connected to in Romania had recently picked up a little dog that they thought was a Chihuahua cross. Like so many others, he had been dumped at a railway station to await his fate. Hessa explained that it was not until the rescuers returned to their rescue that they realised that this little dog was unable to walk. Instead, he could only shuffle around on his forearms, which were by now sore and bleeding. They believed that the little dog had been born with severe birth deformities. My heart immediately went out to this poor little dog, which I later learned was a little boy, aged around six months old.

However, it was not until I saw his photo that I instantly knew that this little boy had just found himself a home. It was heart-breaking to see how terribly thin and dirty he was.

I immediately told Hessa that I would love to adopt him and see if there was anything that I could do to help him.

However, Hessa believed that it would be better for me to foster him to begin with, so that she could be involved in the decision making. I agreed that fostering him first did make more sense and so Hessa decided to bring him over to the UK to begin his new life as soon as possible.

Of course, every dog needs a name to go on their passport and so the next step was to choose a name for this little boy. That was easier said than done because whenever I tried to choose a name for this little sweetheart, I could only come up with all the usual ones and I knew that this little boy needed a special name.

It was for this reason that I decided to search the internet for inspiration.

I began by searching through the lists of Romanian names but nothing really jumped out at me. Next, I began looking at the lists of boys' names in general, still nothing.

It was at this point that I began to think about his character. Hessa had sent me a few videos of him. He was certainly feisty, and cheeky, but the one characteristic that really defined this little boy was the fact that he was a fighter.

This got me searching for names with the definition: strong, fighter, soldier, or warrior. Suddenly, I came across a name which I believed was absolutely perfect for him: Arlo, which, according to several websites, meant strong, guarded and protected.'[2]

This little boy was definitely a strong little dog, a real fighter, and as he was found and rescued, I believe he was being protected by his Guardian Angels.

So, Arlo it was.

When I told Hessa, however, she said that the name made him sound like a yogurt, but I would not be swayed. I liked the name Arlo and thought that it suited him perfectly, and I was not going to change my mind.

CHAPTER 2

Nothing is Ever Easy

For anyone trying to rescue a dog from abroad, the process is never easy. First, there are the vaccinations that every dog travelling into the UK from abroad have to receive by law. Although many rescues insist on their dogs having a wide range of vaccinations, the only required vaccination is the Rabies vaccine.

Next, all of the dogs that are being adopted abroad need to undergo various veterinary checks. They also need to be neutered if they are over the age of six months. Many rescues are also insisting that dogs coming into the UK from abroad have been previously tested for various parasites and diseases caused by ticks. However this is not a legal requirement.

Finally, each dog has to have a microchip and a passport.

When a dog is ready to travel, a place on the transport has to be arranged, booked and paid for, usually by the rescue.

Because Arlo was travelling to the UK from Europe; he was booked to travel by minibus. These minibuses are often referred to as the *'Happy Bus'*, for obvious reasons. All the minibuses transporting dogs

Here is an example of a 'Happy Bus'

are air-conditioned and contain several rows of crates. Each of the crates is made as comfortable as possible for the dogs and they all contain bowls for food and water. Several members of staff travel alongside the dogs to see to their needs at all times. The dogs are provided with fresh food and water and have their crates cleaned out regularly en route.

All the staff on the minibus, and anyone who is transporting dogs, cats and ferrets from abroad, have to follow a set of guidelines laid out by Defra.[3]

Defra Explained

Defra has a set of government guidelines that everyone, including rescues, has to follow if they are transporting dogs and cats into the UK, from Europe.

These rules include guidelines covering the following:

- Where you are travelling from
- Passports and health documents
- Microchip
- Rabies vaccination, booster and blood tests
- Tapeworm treatment

- Guide dogs and assistance dogs
- Approved routes
- Bringing more than five animals
- Arriving in Great Britain
- Complaints and help

As part of the defra ruling, when a rescue dog arrives in Great Britain, it has to remain in the rescue, foster home or boarding kennels for 48 hours. This is to give all of the dogs time to desensitise and get used to their new surroundings after their long and stressful journey.

On November 15, 2020, my darling little Arlo, who I had already fallen in love with, was lifted onto the transport to begin his long journey to the UK by his wonderful rescuer, Stefan.

Once you know that your dog has boarded the transport, every minute feels like an hour and every hour feels like a lifetime.

While Arlo and the other dogs were travelling, I decided to spend my time walking around our local pet store, purchasing everything a puppy could ever dream of.

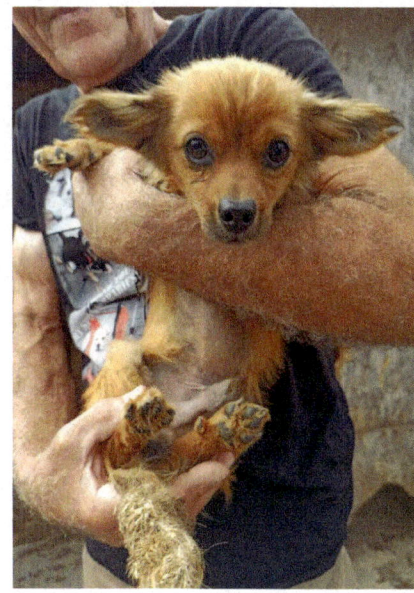

I must have looked at my phone a million times, waiting for that elusive message. Suddenly, my phone went off. I must have jumped six feet up into the air. However, instead of the good news that I was expecting, the news was not good.

Unfortunately, just as Arlo's transport had arrived in France, the UK government had decided to put a ban on all dogs that had been rescued from Romania coming in to the country

My heart sank, what an earth was going to happen to all the dogs that were already on their way?

It appeared that no one knew and the internet was awash with speculation.

However, after reading all the available documentation, it appeared that the UK government had not mentioned any legislation regarding the dogs that were currently being transported. If their ban also included these dogs, then this could mean that poor little Arlo, and two of the other dogs being rescued by Hessa, would be forced to remain in France until the ban was lifted.

While Hessa was frantically trying to find out whether or not these dogs would be allowed to be brought into the UK, I was going out of my mind with worry.

Poor little Arlo, he was only six months old and very disabled; I could only sit and imagine how frightened he must be feeling.

Fortunately, after about four hours of Hessa frantically trying to get through to the telephone helpline which had been set up by the UK government, she phoned me with the good news. The government's ban did not include the dogs that were already on their way. She informed me that the transport had been allowed to board the train in France and little Arlo was finally on his way through the Eurotunnel.

On hearing this fantastic news, everything just became too much for me and I collapsed in tears. My darling little Arlo would finally arrive in the UK later that day.

CHAPTER 3

Arlo Arrives at Hessa's Homeless Hounds

After an exceptionally long and tiring journey, Arlo, along with two other totally exhausted little dogs, finally arrived at *Hessa's Homeless Hounds*, in the early hours of the morning of November 18, 2020.

Like all the rescue dogs that arrive at Hessa's, Arlo was dirty, smelly and totally exhausted after his long journey. After a quick cuddle,

a bowl of food and a drink, he, like his two travel companions, settled down to their first ever night in a comfortable bed.

I often wonder what goes through a dog's mind when they realise that they are truly safe for the first time in their lives. I wonder what they think when they arrive at their destination and are shown love and kindness before being fed and offered the chance to snuggle into what is probably the first ever warm and comfortable bed they have ever had.

From the moment that I knew Arlo had arrived, I was keen to find out exactly when I would be allowed to pick him up. However, as things turned out, the wait would be much longer than I had hoped for.

Hessa had Decided to Get Arlo Scanned Locally

The next morning, Hessa used her time to assess Arlo's disabilities before phoning me to say that she had decided to arrange for Arlo to be scanned nearer to her, to save time and money.

Although I was initially disappointed, I could understand where she was coming from, and so, with a heavy heart, I reluctantly agreed. Sadly, she had also decided that her rescue was no place for a little dog like Arlo because he was very small and extremely disabled, and she therefore decided to ask her friend, Michelle, to foster him for a few weeks.

Michelle is a very close friend of Hessa's who has been involved with her rescue on a daily basis, for years.

Although I was extremely upset and worried that Hessa would ultimately decide not to allow me to foster Arlo after his scans, I tried to be brave and believe that whatever the outcome, Hessa only had Arlo's best interests at heart.

It was wonderful to see the regular updates of Arlo enjoying his new life in the UK, and I could see that he was being very well cared for at Michelle's.

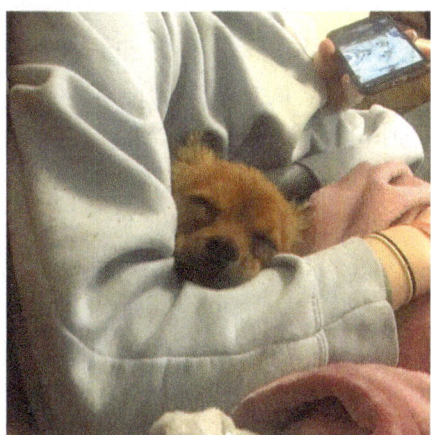 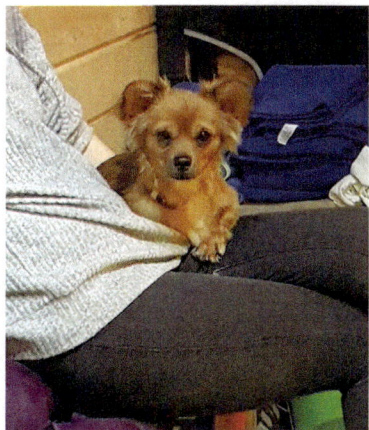

Fundraising and Introducing Arlo to the World

From the moment I first heard about little Arlo's plight, I began thinking of ways that I could raise the funds needed for his treatment.

I had already shown the photos and x-rays that I had received from the vets in Romania to my own vet to get his professional opinion on Arlo's deformities.

He said that without actually seeing Arlo for himself, it was very difficult for him to give an accurate diagnosis. He told me that, in his professional opinion, if anything could be done at all surgically for Arlo, and it was a big if, it was likely to cost well over £20,000.

Undeterred by this news, I decided that the best course of action was to open a facebook page called: *Arlo's New Beginning*. [4] This was to first and foremost introduce the World to little Arlo and update readers on Arlo's progress. The platform would then enable me to post various fundraising events, such as raffles, auctions and anything else that I could think of, to raise the £20,000 plus that was needed to fund Arlo's treatment.

The x-rays of Arlo's legs were much worse that we had all expected and I knew that none of this was going to be easy but I was determined that I was going to do my absolute best to give this little boy the very best life that I could.

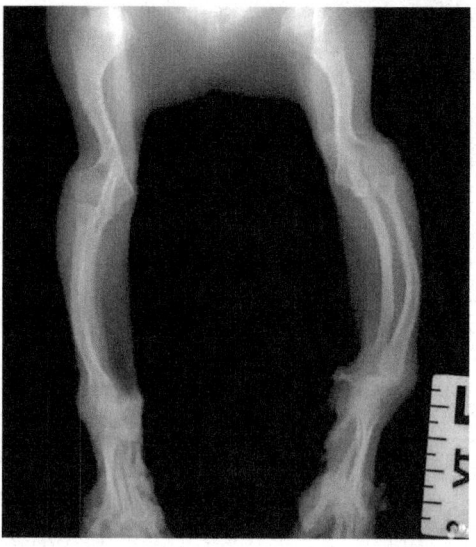

However, being a complete novice at fundraising, I had no idea how I was going to raise this amount of money. Fortunately, my best friend, Linda Cox, came to the rescue and, after many hours discussing our options, we realised that before we could raise any money at all, we needed to get either good quality items that we could sell or some decent prizes for people to win.

I decided that we should put out a plea on social media and ask all my friends and family if they had any unwanted gifts that they would be willing to donate. The response was phenomenal. It appeared that I was not the only one to have fallen in love with little Arlo.

Within days, gifts flooded in and the fundraising began. It was absolutely wonderful to see just how many people were willing to help Arlo have the treatment that he required and hopefully enable him to stand tall for the first time in his life.

I had gifts of makeup, perfume, toys, china and one lady gave me everything that she and her partner had collected from a house clearance.

One of Arlo's followers went on a sponsored diet. She managed to not only lose the weight that she had hoped to lose but raise a whopping £500 in the process. Another supporter was so moved by Arlo's story that she had one side of her head shaved to raise money for Arlo.

During those first few weeks of fundraising, I was often moved to tears by people's kindness and generosity. I just could not believe just how many people were willing to help us, not only by donating such wonderful gifts to help Arlo but the absolute outpouring of love that was shown to us by complete strangers.

CHAPTER 4

A Surprise Phone Call and Meeting Arlo for the First Time

The plan had always been that I would pick up Arlo from Hessa's after Christmas. However, towards the end of November, I received a phone call which I will remember for the rest of my life.

Out of the blue, Hessa phoned me to ask whether or not I would like to pick up Arlo. I could not believe it. I was totally shocked and so excited. In fact, I was so excited that I could not even form a proper sentence because, unbeknown to Hessa, not only was my mind racing like a racehorse being released onto the track at the Grand National but I was smiling from ear to ear, like a Cheshire cat.

I could not believe it. Suddenly, after all the months of preparation and anticipation, not to mention the one hundred and one ups and downs, I was actually going to have my beautiful little boy in time for Christmas. I could not have been happier. It was the absolute best Christmas present that anyone could have ever given me.

I doubt very much if anybody reading this book will ever understand how passionate I am, and always have been, about rescuing disadvantaged and neglected dogs, many of whom have been through the types of trauma that Arlo had been through.

It's difficult to describe how their stories move me to the very core of my being and how deep down I had always been looking for a special little dog that I could really nurture and help lead the life they deserve.

I believe that God answered my prayers and guided me in the right direction because I cannot think of any other reason why I would have contacted Hessa on that particular day. After all, little Minnie had been looking for a home for a very long time and I had not enquired about her before.

A close friend once said to me that you never have to go looking for the perfect little dog because the right little dog will always find a way to find you. He told me that it is for that reason that you never have to look for them because they will always know how to find you at exactly the right time.

Thinking back, he must have been right because I now believe that the reason that I had never contacted Hessa about Minnie before was because Minnie was not the right little dog for me.

I now know this for certain because Hessa had been caring for Minnie for many months before I decided to enquire about her and yet from the moment I heard about little Arlo, I knew without hesitation that no matter how thin and crumpled his little body was, he was just perfect.

Although I was saddened by his extremely poor condition, it did not matter to me that he could not walk, and that his little legs might never be able to support his weight, and that they were covered in open sores from shuffling along in the mud for many months on his forearms, because I knew with every fibre of my being that with care, love and determination, in time, Arlo was going to be the perfect little dog for me.

I knew instantly that I just wanted to be able to cuddle him and tell him that from now on I was going to be his forever Mum and I was going to do everything in my power to protect him and give him the best life ever.

I wanted to tell him about all the adventures that we were going to have together and all the exciting places that we were going to visit. I wanted to explain to him how one day we would visit the best experts and vets that money could buy, and that those experts, using their expertise and knowledge, would try to fix his wonky little legs and hopefully help him to stand tall.

Little did I know exactly how difficult that was going to be, because fixing Arlo was never going to be easy.

Arranging to Bring Arlo Home for the First Time

As I do not have a car and Hessa lives a very long way away from me, I had to arrange for someone to help me to collect Arlo. Fortunately, I have an enormous number of very good friends to help me.

As soon as I mentioned that I was going to pick up Arlo, my friend Helen Lomax offered to give both my best friend Linda Cox (or Lyn as she prefers to be called, who had insisted on coming to pick him up), and myself, a lift.

Everything was set for 28th November.

That day could not arrive soon enough but in the meantime I continued to raise as much money as I possibly could. To enable us to raise the funding required, Lyn and I did auctions, raffles, a GoFundMe and several other social media fundraisers, and by the time Arlo was due to be picked up, we had raised nearly £5,000.

Eventually, the day that I had been waiting for arrived. We decided to take Patsy Lou, who is another one of Hessa's dogs that I had previously adopted from her, and Reily, because he is so friendly and easy going.

I cannot begin to put into words how excited I was. Of course I was a little apprehensive but I pushed all of these feelings to one side because deep down I knew without hesitation that fostering this little boy was the right thing for me to do.

The journey seemed to take forever and, considering how excited we all were, we were exceptionally quiet because we were all lost in our own thoughts. Even the dogs appeared to know that we were all about to embark on a new adventure that was going to change our lives forever.

Due to the distance, we decided to stop around half way for a coffee and to give the dogs a toilet break and time to stretch their legs. This was a welcome break and a distraction from the building tension.

As we approached Hessa's house my emotions were all over the place, and even though I was really excited to be able to finally meet my new little dog, I also felt extremely tearful.

Hessa Cuddling Patsy Lou

When we arrived, Hessa came to the door to greet us followed by a large number of excited dogs in all shapes and sizes, all desperate to say hello and find out who we were.

I feel at this point that I need to explain that Hessa's rescue is unlike any other rescue that I have ever been to. Hessa treats all of the dogs as if they were her own. There are no lines of crates with scared little faces peering out through the bars. Instead, the dogs are all free to roam and explore their environment.

While cuddling Patsy Lou, who she had not seen for a number of years, Hessa told us that she would phone Michelle to get her to fetch Arlo down to the house.

While we waited, I began to pet all the beautiful rescue dogs that she had in her care. Suddenly, Lyn shouted 'Oh my goodness, here he comes'. I turned round to see one of the tiniest, scruffiest dogs that I have ever seen, shuffling towards me. His tail wasn't wagging like a normal dog, it just appeared to go round and round, like a helicopter propeller and his tail has continued to do this ever since.

Full of emotion, I bent down and picked him up, tears rolling down my face. He had the biggest brown eyes that I had ever seen. He just looked at me, as if he was checking me out, before sighing deeply and resting his little head onto my shoulder while nestling into my neck. It was as if he knew that I was his special person who had come to rescue him and take care of him forever.

Amazingly, Arlo still goes to sleep in this position to this day.

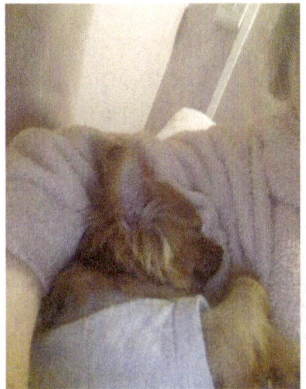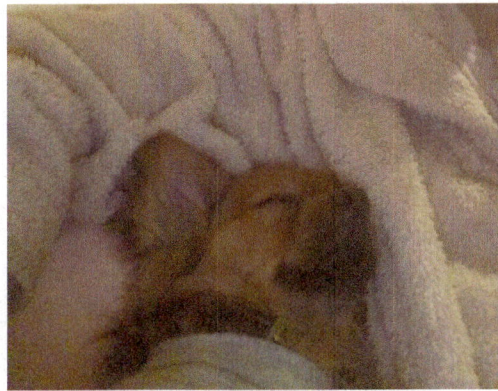

I remember thinking to myself how awfully tiny and thin he was. Of course, before we left for our long journey home, Lyn and Helen wanted a quick cuddle as well. Patsy Lou and Reily had decided that they were going to check out the other dogs while I filled in the necessary paperwork.

After taking a few quick photos and giving Hessa a big hug and a kiss, I put Arlo in the smallest harness and collar that the pet shops sold and boarded the car for our long journey home.

On our way back, we again stopped at a service station so that the three dogs could have a toilet break and stretch their legs.

It was decided that, due to my own disabilities, Helen and I would walk Patsy Lou and Reily, and that Lyn would walk Arlo on an area of grass at the other side of the car park.

Lyn gently picked Arlo up, carried him across the car park and put him down on the grass.

When she came back, she was full of emotion. She explained how he had just shuffled along using his arms and had cocked his leg as if he was a completely normal little dog.

It was at this point that I decided that no matter what happened to Arlo in the future, I would always treat him as a completely normal little dog and that is exactly what I have done.

CHAPTER 5

Arlo Begins his New Life with his Foster Family

When I arrived home it was late and I was greeted at the door by three very curious and excited dogs. After giving them all a cuddle and saying a big thank you to Jane Hills, who had been caring for them all day, I took them all outside to meet their new brother.

Due to the fact that I had fostered many dogs over the years, this was nothing new to them and they just gave him a good sniff before standing back and watching him from afar. After all the dogs had been acquainted with each other, I took them inside for their dinner.

As we have a large step, I gently picked Arlo up and took him into the kitchen with the others. After all the dogs had been fed, and Lyn and Helen had gone home, I let the dogs back into the garden. It was great watching little Arlo sniffing and exploring his new environment.

Once the dogs had relieved themselves, I brought them all in before lifting my precious little boy into a special crate that I had made up for him and it was not long before he climbed into his very own soft little bed and fell asleep.

I would like to add at this point, that I do not usually crate my dogs at night but I felt that Arlo needed to be kept safe, due to his extremely fragile condition. Most of my dogs sleep on my bed at night and I did not want Arlo to attempt to jump onto my bed, to be with the others, during the night.

After watching television and having something to eat, I decided to go up to bed myself, and plan exactly what I was going to do to help Arlo have the best care and treatment possible.

It was for this reason that I found it difficult to sleep that night. Even though I was extremely tired, sleep was the last thing on my mind because suddenly, it began to dawn on me exactly what I had taken on. I began to realise that it was one thing agreeing to foster a little dog like Arlo and another one entirely to care for him full time.

Arlo Soon Proved that he Was a Very Determined Dog

During the next few weeks, Arlo decided to prove to us all just how determined and independent he really was. Within days, he had

somehow managed to master running up and down the steps that I had bought him to get on and off the sofa with.

However, he very quickly became bored of using the steps and decided that he was no different to any of my other dogs. Before I knew what was happening, he was leaping on and off of the sofa, doing his version of a flying squirrel impression.

If I tried to correct him, he would just tilt his head on one side, give me a cheeky little look, and carry on regardless.

There was no stopping him, he was so fast. If the doorbell rang, off he would fly, barking and leaping around as if he owned the place. He soon discovered that by being so small, his bark was nowhere near as loud as the other dogs, so he began to howl and scream at the top of his voice to make sure that he could be heard.

Sadly, this is something that he continues to do today, much to everyone's annoyance.

Worried that he would get hurt in his various attempts to prove himself, I decided to surround my whole sofa with yoga mats in an effort to cushion his fall. This was something that worked extremely well for Arlo but it wasn't really the look I was aiming to achieve for my lounge.

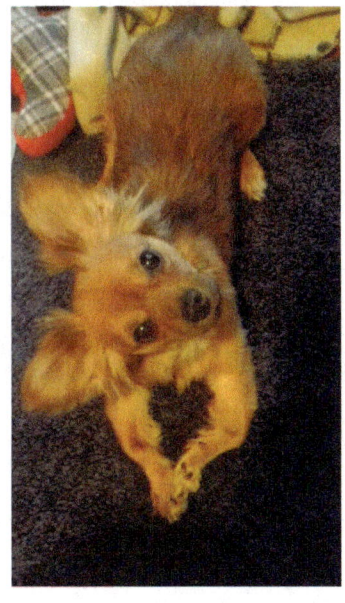

It was for this reason I decided that I would ask a friend of mine if she would be able to make him a couple of little padded vests to protect him from injury. Fortunately she, like the majority of his growing online fan club, was only too happy to oblige. She proceeded to make him two beautiful handmade little padded bomber jacket type vests which fastened around his neck and around his back.

To be honest, once Arlo began to wear his little bomber jackets, he began to look less and less like a little dog, and more and more like a Ninja Turtle Warrior.

After he had been living with me for about a week, I decided it was time to take him out for a walk. Lyn and I decided to take him to the park with Patsy Lou and Reily for his first walk. We decided not to take Meisha, Shelby and Scottie because they were too big and we thought that they might overwhelm Arlo.

It was decided that Lyn should lead walk Patsy Lou and Reily, while I carried Arlo in my arms. When we arrived, I gently put Arlo down on the soft grass and just let him explore. Hessa had advised me to let him explore the park off lead because she believed that it was not possible for him to outrun me.

Personally, I think that she may have underestimated this little one because he had decided that he was going to run and play with his siblings and there was absolutely nothing that I or anyone else could do to stop him.

I will never forget that first outing. Before playing with the others, Arlo made his first ever attempt to stand on his exceptionally wobbly, deformed little legs, to try to cock his leg and pee up the waste paper bin. Sadly, his first attempt failed and ended up with him face down in the dirt. However, Arlo was not a little dog to give up easily and he decided that he would try again but this time he would try leaning his body against the bin. Success. Arlo had managed to defy all the odds and pee up the bin like any other little dog.

He then decided to run off to play chase with his siblings. Round and round they all went, screaming and barking at the top of their voices.

A few onlookers came over to me to ask me what was wrong with Arlo's legs and once I had explained, the majority of them really understood and bent down to give him a stroke. However, there are always one or two who decide that it is their duty to inform you that what you are doing is cruel and that dogs like Arlo should be put out of their misery and put to sleep.

I had absolutely no intention of having any one of my dogs put to sleep and I believed that the sooner that the locals got used to that fact, the better.

I will never forget one lady who said that looking at Arlo's little legs all twisted, made her feel sick. I turned round to her practically in tears and said, *"Look love, no one is asking for you to look at his legs, are they?"* and with that I picked Arlo up, gave her a filthy look and gave him the biggest hug I could, and made my way towards the gate.

Of course, an awful lot has happened since Arlo's first walk in the park but I will never forget that very first walk and the joy I felt watching him run around like a normal little dog with his two siblings.

Normality comes in many forms. For me, Arlo is and always has been normal, he is just a regular little dog trying to enjoy life the best way that he can. Yes, he has wobbly legs that tend to collapse when he tries to stand up but for Arlo, that is his normality. Like the majority of disabled dogs out there, they do not know that they are disabled; they just continue to enjoy life the only way they know how.

My Cheeky Chappie

CHAPTER 6

Arlo Meets a UK Vet for the First Time

After Arlo had been with me for about two weeks, I decided that it was time to take him to meet my vet and have a check-up. Due to the fact that I do not drive, I contacted a very close friend of mine, Mr. Derek Spooner, who runs the only Pet Ambulance service in the area. Once we had negotiated a time and date that suited everyone, the appointment was booked.

Fortunately, the vet that I go to, the Storrington branch, of the *Arun Veterinary group*[5], is one of the leading veterinary practices in the area. They are not only excellent in veterinary care but they have a wide range of very talented and highly qualified surgeons and veterinary staff working for them. Each and every one of them cares passionately about all of the pets

that are registered there. It does not matter whether the animal that they are caring for is a mouse, a rabbit or even a Great Dane, the same level of care and attention is given to each one of them.

They all knew all about Arlo in advance because from the moment that I knew that I was going to foster him, I had kept them fully updated with photos, scans and x-rays, so that they were all well versed in exactly what his disabilities were, and they could not wait to meet him.

However, I do not think that any of us were prepared in any way for that first meeting.

As the surgery was still following the COVID 19 protocol, Lyn and I were not allowed to go into the building and so we were met outside by one of their leading orthopaedic surgeons, who sadly, is no longer at Arun vets.

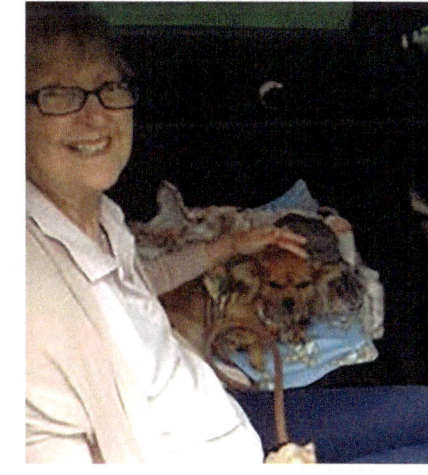

I do not think that I will ever forget the look of tenderness and love on his face the very first day that he met

Arlo. As he ever so gently took this tiny, scared little dog out of my arms, he said: *"Hi little man, now what have we got here?"* He then proceeded to walk very slowly towards the surgery with my little Arlo held very close to his chest as if he was the most precious little dog in the world.

I will never forget the way that he held my little boy and I will remember his kindness towards Arlo for the rest of my life because as he walked away, he continued to softly reassure him that he was not going to hurt him and that from now on, everything was going to be just fine.

It was at that moment, that I knew in my heart, that every choice and decision that was going to be made for Arlo by my vet was going to be made carefully and professionally. I knew without a doubt that each and every one of them would consider all the facts very carefully, before making any decision that could affect Arlo's health and wellbeing and that they would always make my little dog's welfare their top priority.

Arlo's Assessment

After fully assessing Arlo and introducing him to every single vet, nurse, physiotherapist and receptionist that worked at the practice, he and the physiotherapist, Becky Rawlingson, brought Arlo back into the car park.

Becky Rawlingson

He told me that the entire team had totally fallen in love with Arlo and they all believed that it would be possible to correct his legs. However, although they believed that Arlo could be helped, they also believed that he would need an intensive course of physiotherapy to get him as strong as possible because as it stood, Arlo's little legs were extremely fragile and were already causing him to suffer from an awful lot of pain.

At this point Becky, the physiotherapist, explained to me that Arlo could not be helped using splints, as his bones were no longer soft like those of a puppy. She believed that his treatment should begin by having regular massages and laser sessions, to strengthen his legs and free him of any pain that he was suffering.

The vet then went on to explain to me that after his course of physiotherapy, Arlo would need to be referred to a specialist referral unit for a full assessment. He told me that even though Arlo had already undergone a series of x-rays and scans in Romania, he would need to undergo further x-rays and a CT scan because, over the months, his legs and how he used them would have changed. He explained that his treatment would not be cheap as the x-rays and scans alone would cost in excess of £3000.

He continued that if the experts then decided that Arlo was a good candidate for surgery and that it was indeed possible for them to help Arlo, this surgery could end up costing me tens of thousands of pounds.

I told him that it didn't matter how much it cost, I wanted Arlo to get the best help and support that money could buy.

At this point, I would like to explain that although Hessa's Homeless Hounds had asked to be involved with all the decision making for Arlo, they were not in a position to financially support him or any other dog needing this level of care. This is because they are an extremely small rescue and are totally reliant on public donations.

I told the vet that I had already been fundraising for months and that to-date I had already raised in excess of £8,000. It was my aim to just keep going until I could afford to help Arlo and pay for any surgery and treatment that this little boy needed.

He said that he understood and that, in the meantime, he and his team would do everything possible to help Arlo.

After I thanked them all for their time, I proceeded to book Arlo in for his first physiotherapy session and pay for the consultation.

We left the practice with renewed hope, knowing that one day, after a lot of dedication and hard work, there was a possibility that Arlo would be able to stand tall, just like any other little dog.

CHAPTER 7

The Hard Work Begins

As Arlo's first appointment at the vets was during December, the next major event for us all was Christmas.

We had decided that the fastest and easiest way to raise some much needed finance at this time of year was to raffle a hamper. Once again, we decided that it would be a good idea to put out a plea online, for the various items that we needed to put in the hamper.

I now see that we had totally underestimated the huge impact that this little dog was making on the internet. It appeared that everyone had totally fallen in love with Arlo and his little crooked legs.

Within days, I was inundated with gifts of chocolate, cakes, tins of biscuits, fruit, ham, Christmas crackers, bottles of wine, and a whole range of other wonderful items. In fact, due to the vast quantity of fabulous goodies that people had so kindly donated, we were able to make, not one but three absolutely huge Christmas hampers, to raffle.

I cannot even begin to tell you how proud we both were of those three wonderful hampers that we were able to raffle that Christmas. We both knew that these hampers alone would help us gain much needed funding for Arlo's surgery.

As Lyn had previously worked in a gift shop and she was the artistic one out of the two of us, I decided that I would leave all the decorating of the hampers to her and I was absolutely amazed at the fantastic effort that she put into them.

All three hampers were better than we could have ever imagined, and I would like to thank everyone who donated such kind and thoughtful gifts to put in them.

Due to everyone's kindness, these three hampers raised well in excess of £500, which was a fantastic amount of money at such a difficult time of the year.

We also decided that as it was Christmas, we would start taking a wide range of wonderful photos of Arlo, to make a calendar that we could sell the following Christmas.

Looking back, I believe that we knew from the very beginning that raising such an enormous amount of money, in such a short amount of time, was never going to be easy. However, to this day, I do not think we really appreciated just how difficult the fundraising was going to be.

On reflection, I have to laugh at some of our efforts, which I have to admit, were totally off the scale madness. For example, during the UK government's lockdown, in the early part of 2021, we decided to hold an online table top sale.

Of course, at the time I do not think we had even given a thought to how this was actually going to work.

Over the months, we had accumulated a large amount of china, soft toys, books, DVDs etc, which we believed we could sell on large tables in my back garden.

Naively, we decided that if the public were unable to go to regular table top sales, holding one online would be huge fun and attract an awful lot of online attention.

Of course, we had forgotten to take into account that my garden was not only very uneven, it had the most enormous magnolia tree situated in the middle of it. This, along with six inquisitive dogs, made setting up the tables near on impossible.

Even when we did manage to get tables set up, we found that because we were unable to price things up individually, we had to price things up in sections and because I had no idea how to do the table top live, I had to keep putting photos up.

Needless to say the whole sale was a total disaster, we made around £20 and all ended up totally exhausted.

Easter Chocolate Extravaganza

Of course, not all of our efforts went down like lead balloons. One of our all-time great successes was the chocolate extravaganza which we set up at Easter.

We asked everyone on our social media pages and all our family and friends, to donate Easter eggs and anything chocolatey, to help us to raise money for Arlo. Well, let's face it, who doesn't enjoy binging on chocolate at Easter?

I decided that I would also try to get some of the major chocolate manufacturers involved. Sadly, many of the major companies, manufacturing some of the UK's best loved chocolate, were not interested in helping little Arlo and judging by their curt emails, obviously did not believe that Arlo was a worthy enough cause for them.

However, not all companies were so dismissive. One local company, *Montezuma's Luxury Chocolate Gifts* [6], did decide to back our cause

and sent us the most beautiful chocolate hamper to raffle.

Their generosity and kindness really did restore our faith in the retail industry and gave us the courage to ask other manufacturers and local retail outlets to get on board.

I had never seen so much chocolate in my whole life. Just about every one of my friends and online followers got behind Arlo, and sent us chocolate to fill up our hampers. We ended up with ten wonderful hampers to raffle which, once again, Lyn lovingly decorated and made her personal works of art.

Once again we raised an enormous amount of money to put towards Arlo's surgery and I would like to thank everyone who got involved.

Although we were raising large sums of money through our own fundraisers, other fundraising groups were also getting on board to support Arlo. One group in particular, *Chihuahua Support All Paws*,[7] run by a wonderful lady, Eve Smith, had fallen in love with Arlo and as a consequence, had decided that their group would love to support him.

At the time, I had never heard of them and was surprised to learn that they were trying to get in touch with me. When we all finally caught up with each other, I was shocked to discover that they were not only offering to support Arlo financially but were also offering to buy him the necessary equipment to aid in his progress.

This equipment included a stroller, to help us take him out and about, therapies, such as physiotherapy and hydrotherapy, various crates, bedding, steps, puppy pads, and a wide range of slings and support aids, that all have been necessary to support Arlo throughout his journey.

Arlo particularly loved the stroller and enjoyed being taken out in it at every opportunity.

I now totally believe that if it had not been for groups like *Chihuahua Support All Paws* offering to help me to not only support Arlo but help raise the finance necessary for his surgery and all the various aids that he required, it would all have been so much more difficult.

I would like to thank *Chihuahua Support All Paws* and the many other groups who have supported Arlo, many of which I will mention further on in this book, for all their hard work and for their amazing support and dedication over the years.

Photos and Summer Fun

One of the most exciting things that happened during the first year that we fostered Arlo was that Eve Smith, the founder of *Chihuahua Support All Paws,* came to visit.

This was not an easy task as Eve lived in the North of England and we lived in the South. It took her and her work colleague around seven hours to reach our house but they were absolutely determined to see our little man for themselves.

Of course, like everyone who met Arlo, Eve fell instantly in love with his enduring ways, and wanted to put him in her bag and take him home. This was something that I made very clear was not going to happen.

They were both absolutely amazed at just how agile he was, even with his two wonky front legs and they couldn't help smiling at all of his cheeky antics. Arlo, of course, was not backward in coming forward and was desperate to show her just how far he had come in the few months that he had been in our care.

He proved that not only could he stand on his own four legs like a big boy, for up to four seconds, but that he could also shuffle down the beach at the rate of knots to catch his brothers and sisters.

We all had so much fun that day, with Arlo, of course, being the centre of attention, something that he loved more than anything else in the world, and it gave us the chance to take some fantastic photos.

When she and her work colleague were leaving, they vowed that they would continue to raise money to help Arlo through their group and they have both been true to their word.

The one thing that Arlo loved was posing for the camera and this was something we had decided to take full advantage of. We took photos of his antics at every given opportunity.

I loved dressing him up in a wide range of doggie outfits so that we could take some absolutely fantastic photos for our forthcoming calendar.

Usually, I do not agree with dressing dogs up but I felt that to get the best photos and to make him look even more enduring for the calendar (if that was actually possible), dressing him up would make it all so much more fun.

Every month, we planned our photo very carefully, so that we could get the best possible 12 monthly photos of Arlo. I cannot even begin to tell you all just how much fun we had that first year.

Although I took most of the photos for the calendar myself, I also used professional photographer, Ollie, from *Paws and Claws Photography*,[8] to take some professional photos as well.

One of my favourite months with Arlo was March. Coming from Romania and being found in such an appalling condition, it was blatantly obvious that little Arlo had never seen grass, let alone experienced the beauty of flowers.

I will never forget his little face, as he began to explore his new environment. One of the funniest moments was when he came face to face with a Bluebell for the first time. Being so small, the bluebells appeared to tower above him like giant trees and in springtime, my garden grows a carpet of bluebells.

That first spring, Arlo just stood at the back door, with a look of sheer joy on his face, smelling the air. As he gradually ventured outside, he just stood by some bluebells, and moved his eyes from the bottom of the flower, to the top, as they towered above him like gigantic blue trees in the spring sunshine.

From day one, Arlo has loved flowers and during his first spring with us, he spent much of his time exploring the many bluebells, snowdrops and daffodils that filled my garden.

That year, we took some absolutely amazing photos of him smelling the flowers and just lying in the grass. We used some of the best ones in our calendar.

 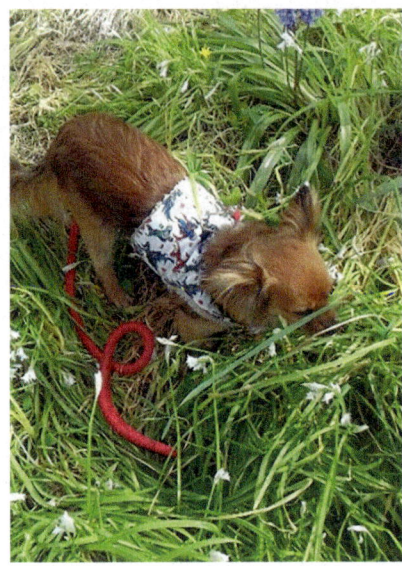

In April, we decided to stage an Easter Rabbit picnic in my garden. However, as we soon found out, us deciding to do something and actually being able to execute it was never going to be as easy as we thought.

We began by laying a beautiful Easter table cloth on the grass, and assembling our pretend picnic. What we had not bargained for was Arlo being absolutely terrified of the giant fluffy rabbit which we were going to use as part of the setting.

Every time we put the cuddly toy anywhere near Arlo, he took flight and just ran, knocking absolutely everything over in his path. This included cups, saucers, Easter eggs and flowers. Of course, the first time that he did it, we found this absolutely hilarious but we quickly learned that our best option was to stage the rabbit a safe distance away, so as not to frighten him too much.

Eventually, after a lot of hard work we got some amazing photos and even managed to get Arlo to look as if he was enjoying the experience.

Amazingly, the photos turned out to be absolutely beautiful and, as amateurs, Lyn and I were really proud of ourselves.

For the months of June and July, we decided to stage Arlo going away on a holiday. Fortunately, Ollie had taken some amazing photos of Arlo sitting on a suitcase and in a deckchair.

Arlo on his Holidays

We also managed to take some great photos of our little man sitting on the beach and on the rocks.

One day, for fun, we dressed him up in a little sailor outfit and took a photo of him sitting on top of an upturned boat.

To this day, that photo of Arlo dressed up like a sailor, is one of my all-time favourites. He just looked so cute, especially as his hat kept sliding off to one side.

That year, we took so many photos of him out and about and doing things that we never expected him to do. Luckily, Arlo was one of the cutest, most photogenic little dogs I had ever come across, which made things so much easier.

Each month portrayed a different image of Arlo doing something that we believed represented that particular month.

These included his first day at school, Halloween and of course Christmas.

The calendar was a great success, and it went a long way towards helping us to raise even more funds towards Arlo's referral appointment, scans and possible surgery.

Front Page of Our Calender

CHAPTER 9

Arlo is Referred for Surgery

Ever since Arlo attended his first appointment at the vets, he had been receiving weekly physiotherapy and laser therapy from phys-iotherapist, Becky Rawlinson.

One day, Becky came into the reception area and told me Arlo had made amazing progress and that she now believed that Arlo had improved enough to be con-sidered for surgery.

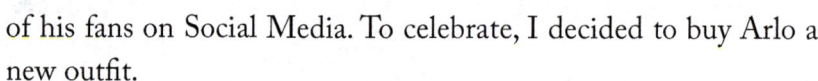

I was absolutely thrilled with the news, and could not wait to tell all of his fans on Social Media. To celebrate, I decided to buy Arlo a new outfit.

I could not believe how far Arlo had come in such a short amount of time and was so proud of my beautiful little boy. I knew that there were no guarantees and that it may not be possible for him to ever be able to run and play like a normal little dog but whatever happened to Arlo in the future, I knew that I had done everything humanly possible to help him achieve the best that he could be.

It was very important that Arlo was referred to exactly the right unit for his condition and so the next decision that we all needed to make was which referral centre would be the best one for Arlo.

After endless conversations with my veterinary team, it was decided that Arlo should be referred to *Anderson Moores Veterinary Specialists*[9], near Winchester.

This was because not only did they have a team of leading ortho-paedic surgeons working for them but, in 2020, I had another dog referred to them in an emergency, with outstanding results.

I cannot begin to tell you how excited we all were the day that all of Arlo's x-rays, information and medical history were forwarded to *Anderson Moores Veterinary Specialists* for review.

Once it was confirmed that they had received all of his information, it was an agonising wait to see if Arlo was a little dog that they would consider for surgery.

At this point, I feel that it is important to explain that, just because a dog is referred to experts for surgery, not all of them will be accepted. This is because sadly, not every dog is suitable due to their age, length of time between injury and referral, and their overall condition.

The day that I received the phone call from *Anderson Moores* had begun like any other. We had taken the dogs out for their morning walk and were at home planning yet another fund raising event. Suddenly, out of the blue, the phone rang.

Although I had been hoping and praying for that call to come, when it finally did come, I could hardly believe that it was actually them. They explained that after having several meetings to discuss Arlo's case, the surgeons had decided that they would love to meet him and discuss his case further.

This news was absolutely fantastic and it took me a while to process the fact that the day that I had hoped and dreamed of for the past year had finally come. After I had eventually calmed down, and had stopped babbling like an idiot down the phone, we set a date for the team at *Anderson Moores* to meet Arlo.

After a long discussion, we decided on the 23rd of August, 2021.

The next thing that I did was to phone Hessa, to let her know the news. Like me, she was really excited and expressed how pleased she was with all his progress. Hessa knew how much work it had taken to get him to this point and how much Arlo had been improving. This was because every week since I began fostering him, I had sent her an update report.

It is very important for anyone fostering a dog, whether it is disabled or not, to give regular updates to the rescue centre that they are fostering from. This is because it helps them to find the very best home that they can when the time comes for the dog to be adopted.

Arlo's Big Day

Due to the fact that I had no transport, I decided I would contact Helen, who had driven us to Hertfordshire to pick Arlo up. Like myself, she was very excited for little Arlo and agreed to take us to Winchester for our appointment.

When the big day finally arrived, we were all extremely excited, although to be honest we did not have a clue what to expect. It was my understanding that after the initial examination, Arlo would go on to have scans, to assess exactly what, if anything, they could do for him.

I had fully expected that if they did believe it was possible to help Arlo, then he would be taken in that day for surgery. However, this could not have been further from the truth.

I had no idea of the vast amount of preparation that would go into helping an extremely complex case like Arlo's but it was not long before these complexities became evident.

When we arrived the centre was still using lockdown ruling, therefore I was not allowed to go in.

After we had booked ourselves in, Mr. Andy Moores, who was not only a partner at *Anderson Moores Veterinary Specialists* but one of their leading orthopaedic surgeons, came to greet us. Due to Arlo's unique disabilities, it was decided not to examine him outside but for Mr. Moores to carry him inside for his examination.

Mr. Moores explained that, after his examination, if the team believed that it was possible to help Arlo, they would then go on to scan him, to see whether or not surgery was, in their professional opinion, an option that they would consider for Arlo.

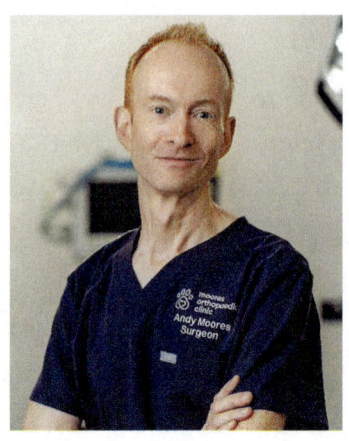

Mr Moores explained that if they did decide to scan Arlo, he would come out and let me know. He told me that he would then run through the risks of the anaesthetic, the pricing, and go through the forms for me to sign if I wanted to go ahead.

I think that letting Arlo be taken into the building by complete strangers was one of the hardest things I have ever had to do, because suddenly he looked so scared, small and vulnerable. I gave him a kiss and told him that his Mummy loved him very much and that he was going to be absolutely fine. A female member of the team stepped forward and took Arlo out of my arms. She could obviously see that I was feeling really emotional and as she took Arlo gently away from me she told me that they would take extra special care of him. She explained that the examination would take about half an hour.

As my eyes filled up with tears, I turned and went slowly back to the car. Lyn and Helen put their arms around me and reassured me that he would be OK. We decided that while we were waiting, we would stretch our legs. I do not know about the others but I think, for me, it was the longest 30 minutes of my life.

Suddenly, the doors opened and Mr. Moores came over to see me. He told me that he had examined Arlo and that he believed that it was possible to help him. He explained to me that they could not help every dog and that for some dogs, surgery was just not an option but in Arlo's case he was young and healthy. He asked me what I was expecting to achieve from the surgery. I explained that I did not believe for one moment that Arlo could be made perfect. I explained that if it was at all possible, I would love Arlo to be up on all four legs and to be able to run and play with his siblings, in whatever way that he could. I told him that I was a realist and that I knew just how disabled Arlo was. I said that if he could help him in any way at all, that that would be enough for me.

Mr. Moores nodded and told me that he did not know whether or not he could help Arlo at all and that he could not make that decision until he and his team had reviewed the scans in full. He explained to me that if it was possible to help Arlo, then it could work out to be very expensive because it involved exceptionally complex surgery. I explained to him that we had already raised approximately £8,500 from our fundraising.

He said that if I wanted to go ahead, although in most cases the risks of the anaesthetic were relatively low, some dogs can suffer an allergic reaction, breathing complications, or, in very rare cases, death. I said that I understood the risks and that I still wanted to proceed.

He told me that if I was absolutely sure, I was to sign the form and that he would phone me when Arlo was ready to be picked up. He said that it would take around three hours to scan Arlo and that he would see me later. After the forms were signed, I paid for the procedure at the desk and we decided to go out to the local garden centre for a coffee while we waited for Arlo.

As we left to make our way to the garden centre, we all had mixed emotions. Although we were very excited for Arlo, we also felt apprehensive about the outcome of the scans and the prospect of Arlo's future on four legs, if indeed it was a possibility. I don't know about the others but I can honestly say that coffee and cake was the last thing on my mind. However, I did find time to buy Arlo a new toy and all of my other little charges some treats.

While I was waiting for Mr. Moores to phone, I decided to phone my friend Jane, to check up on all of my other little dogs that I had left at home. Jane, who was kindly looking after them, said they were absolutely fine and asked me how everything was going. I explained to her about the appointment and she reassured me by telling me that it all sounded very positive and not to worry.

Not long after my phone call to Jane, the phone rang. It was the vets calling to tell me that Arlo had had his scans and that everything had gone to plan and that I could come to collect him. After thanking them, I told the others and we got up to leave. Although we all felt relieved that Arlo was absolutely fine, we were anxious to see whether or not we would receive the news that we were hoping for.

When we got there, we booked in at reception and went back to the car to wait. After about twenty minutes, the door opened and Mr. Moores came over to the car carrying Arlo. As he handed him to me, he told me that he had been a very good dog and that he had been an absolute pleasure to look after.

As I gave Arlo a big hug and a kiss and put him back safely in the car, Mr. Moores said that after reviewing the scans, he felt that it would be possible to help Arlo. He explained that in order to help Arlo, he would need to order specialised guides, plates and cutters to assist him through the surgery. He said that this was because not only did Arlo have exceptionally small bones, his deformities were unique and complex.

To demonstrate exactly what he meant, Mr. Moores showed us Arlo's scans on a screen, He explained that in order for him to know exactly where he needed to cut and realign Arlo's bones, he needed to use the special guides and cutters that would be designed to be exactly the correct shape, measurements and specifications for Arlo.

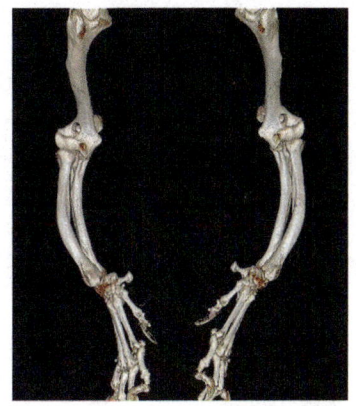

He said that as Arlo's bones were so small, he would also need to have custom made plates manufactured to attach to the bones. He told me that they would also need to fuse Arlo's wrists, due to his unique disabilities.

This was all beginning to sound very complicated and very expensive, but after having it all explained, I knew that if Arlo was to ever be able to stand and walk on all four legs, this was his only chance.

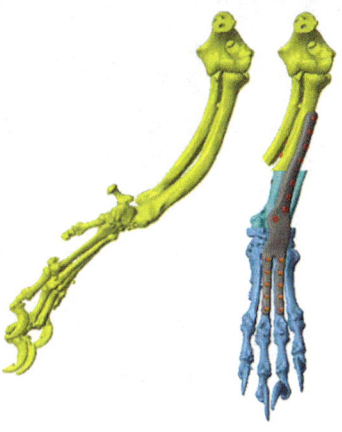

Mr. Moores said that he understood if I needed time to think everything through, that I did not need to make any decisions there and then.

I told him that, realistically, I knew that this was Arlo's only chance of any kind of normality and that I did not need time to think.

I explained that, even though I was only fostering Arlo, I loved him very much and wanted to do everything possible to give him the best life that I could. I continued that I did not feel that it was fair to keep him living the way that he was. His little arms were very sore and if he did not have surgery, he would begin to get infections and could then be at risk of losing his front legs altogether. He told me that he understood and would be in touch very soon with the designs and pricing. I thanked him for everything that he was trying to do for Arlo and walked back to the car with renewed hope and optimism.

As we left, I told the others the news. Like me, they were all really excited for Arlo and the possibility of having him on all four legs. However, we all knew that we would have a lot of hard work ahead of us, raising the extra money required to make our dream for Arlo a reality.

CHAPTER 10

More Fundraising and Hard Work

The next few months were taken up with fundraising. Every week, we tried to find more and more ways of raising money. This was not easy as much of the UK was still using the Covid 19 rules and social interaction restrictions that had been set in place by the government. This meant that large events such as car boot sales and indoor fêtes were not allowed, making normal fundraising events almost impossible.

One of my Facebook friends decided to help Arlo by making a large amount of homemade jam, with fruit from her allotment. This was absolutely fantastic news because I can honestly say that her jam is the most delicious jam that I have ever tasted. As Lyn was our Queen of Packaging, she was assigned to making the jam look as fabulous as it tasted. She was able to come up with some unique ideas to package the jam up to sell. Fortunately, we were able to buy stickers and jam accessories on the internet and this made it very easy for us to advertise and sell the jam through our Facebook page. The jam was an absolute success and we were able to sell all of the jars really easily.

Another one of my friends had been collecting soft toys for another dog rescue to sell at their fair. Sadly, the event was cancelled and due to the lack of funding the rescue had been forced to close down. This left my friend with literally hundreds of soft toys and no one to donate them to.

She asked me if I would be interested in selling them to help Arlo. I thanked her and told her that we would love to sell them. However, I must admit that when they arrived, I was completely taken aback by the sheer quantity of cuddly toys that suddenly arrived on my doorstep. Not one to be put off by a task being too big, I soon had raffles and sales going on all the time and it was not long before the number of toys dwindled to just a few.

I would just like to say that the quality of the toys that she had donated to us was outstanding. The majority of them were original Disney toys, which as you know, are always very popular and easy to sell.

One of the toys that this kind lady had donated was a Harrods Teddy Bear, which we decided to auction. I am thrilled to say that this beautiful bear raised a huge amount of money towards Arlo's fund, which by now was beginning to build up nicely.

Towards the end of the year, and after some of the government's restrictions had been lifted, two very kind sisters who had really taken little Arlo into their heart asked me if I wanted to bring Arlo along to their village club and speak to the members about his story.

Although this was something that I had not done before, I decided that I would go and asked my eldest son Daniel to come along to help me. Daniel agreed and I told the sisters that I would be honoured to come.

This event turned out to be one of the best things that I had ever done. It was so interesting, and the members were really thrilled to meet little Arlo and to hear his story.

I had decided that as Daniel was going to be there to help me, I would take a couple of my other little rescue dogs along to the event as well. I feel that advertising the fact that there are so many wonderful dogs from abroad looking for homes is always a good idea.

I found that some of the elderly people at the event really enjoyed meeting, holding and cuddling my other rescue dogs, while I was speaking about Arlo's story.

Thanks to these two wonderful sisters, this event raised an awful lot of money for Arlo's fund. The money was raised through donations, a raffle and the generosity of the event's organiser, who handed over all of the entrance fees to help towards Arlo's surgery.

Throughout my journey, I have found the outpouring of love for Arlo, from complete strangers, to be extremely heart-warming. After all, he is just one of hundreds of thousands of little dogs needing help to overcome horrendous abuse, injuries and atrocities.

I cannot express how grateful I am to each and every person who has donated to Arlo over the years. It is only through their love and generosity that Arlo is the dog that he is today.

I decided that I would not mention each and every one of these contributors by name because there were so many of them and I did not want to miss anyone out. They all know who they are.

When Arlo joined my family, I had never ever done any fundraising. I went into this journey blind. I had no idea how to raise money nor whether I was going to be able to help Arlo to have the surgery that he desperately needed. I needn't have worried about a thing. As soon as I put Arlo's story onto the internet, the love that was shown towards this little dog was absolutely extraordinary.

Everyone has been absolutely wonderful, which has made my fundraising journey much easier and so much more enjoyable.

Another fundraising support group who helped us to raise money for Arlo was Lime Trees Fundraising, run by Teresa Berry Shambrook, Teresa was another fantastic lady who helped to support Arlo and like Eve she also came to visit us.

We had a lovely day and she too, fell in love with Arlo.

Over the years, it has been lovely to see just how many people were willing to give up their valuable time to visit Arlo and help us to raise the finance required to help

Teresa with Arlo

him. Without each and every one of them, Arlo could never have got the help that he so desperately needed.

Arlo Having Fun

CHAPTER 11

Arlo's Surgery Goes Ahead

On 23rd August, 2021, the staff at Anderson Moores decided to discuss Arlo's scans at a team meeting. This was to see if everyone in the team agreed that it would indeed be possible to operate on Arlo, given his size and complex deformities.

Of course this meant another anxious wait for me as I waited for a definitive answer as to whether or not the surgery could go ahead as planned, and if so, to get a confirmed date.

Three days later, 26th August, 2021, the news we had all been waiting for was confirmed by Mr. Moores's secretary. She told us that the team had decided that it was possible for them to operate on Arlo. However, the operation could not go ahead until November 16th, as Mr. Moores needed to order custom made cutters, plates and 3D models of each leg.

We were ecstatic. Finally, after all the fund raising, tears and hard work, Arlo was going to have the surgery that we had longed for. While we knew that there were no certainties, at least for now we knew that there was hope.

I do not know who cried the most that day but I do know that the tears flowed. The feeling of relief and sheer joy was overwhelming. I glanced over at my little boy struggling to get around on his two bent and deformed front legs, totally oblivious as to why everybody was in tears and it was difficult to believe that because of these wonderful talented surgeons, one day he might be able to walk.

I could not believe it, Arlo was actually going to be given the chance that I had been praying for.

Arlo is Admitted for Surgery

It had been arranged that Arlo would be admitted the day before his operation, as it was too difficult for me to get him to the referral unit before eight in the morning.

So, on 15th November, 2021, we got ourselves ready and set off for Anderson Moores referrals. Arlo travelled to his appointment in his pet carrier, dressed in his latest fashion harness.

We were all full of emotions travelling to Winchester that day. We were of course very excited for Arlo and for this new chapter in Arlo's life; however, our feelings were tinged with sadness for the dog that we were going to lose, the one with the wonky legs and sassy personality, and we all feared what could happen to Arlo if anything should go wrong.

Arriving at Anderson Moores

Although I trusted Mr. Moores, I was still worried that things could go wrong, given the size and fragility of Arlo's legs.

While we were in the waiting room, Arlo decided to do a poo, which of course was totally inappropriate. I guess it was his way of saying that he was not impressed, but we did laugh. The staff were so kind and not phased in the slightest, although we were so embarrassed that we wanted the floor to open up and swallow us. However, as the saying goes… *when you have to go, you have to go.*

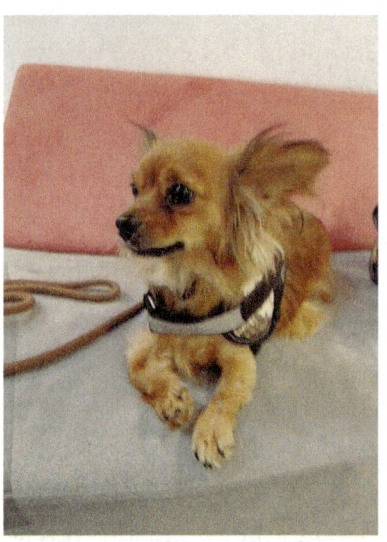

After examining Arlo, Mr. Moores went through the details of the surgery with us using the x-rays and the 3D models that had been made of Arlo's legs. I must admit that the models did make things a lot clearer for me and although it was nerve wracking to see how complex the operation was, all of the staff did their best to put us at ease.

When it was time to hand Arlo over to the staff that were going to care for him for the next few days, it was so difficult. I could see the fear in Arlo's eyes and I just prayed so hard that I was doing the right thing.

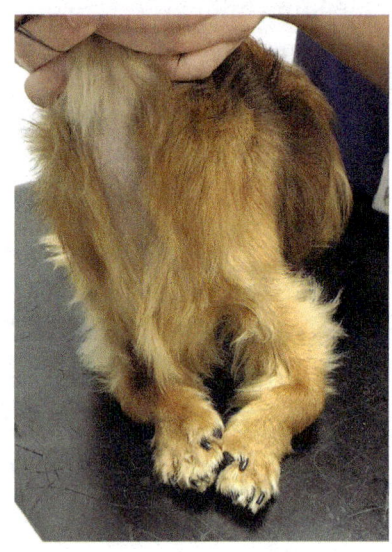

After saying goodbye to Arlo, we decided to go to the garden centre. When we arrived, we saw a little robin that continued to hover around us all day, as if trying to reassure us that everything was going to be absolutely fine. I now believe that robin was from our very dear friend Ailsa Bowman who was in a coma after suffering a catastrophic bleed on the brain, a few days earlier.

Ailsa loved little Arlo so much and had done so much fundraising for him. I now believe that although she was in a coma, she had somehow sent a little robin to watch over Arlo, and this was her way of letting us know that she was here supporting us all and that she would make sure that Arlo would be just fine.

The next day was extremely difficult for me. My mind was on nothing else but my little Arlo. Although deep in my heart, I knew that he was a fighter, I knew that this was going to be a very long and complicated surgery.

It was not until about 6pm that evening that we finally received the call we had been waiting for. Arlo was in recovery and doing well. The operation had gone to plan and had taken exactly seven hours to complete.

Mr. Moores explained that the operation was extremely difficult, as Arlo's bones were so fragile. He asked me whether or not I would like to see photos of the surgery. I said yes I would love to but perhaps not the really gory ones.

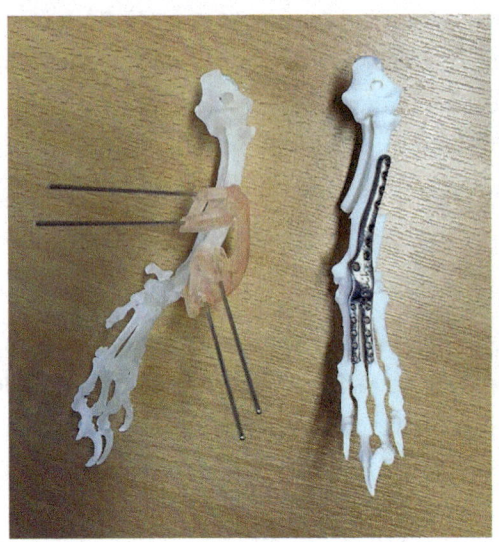
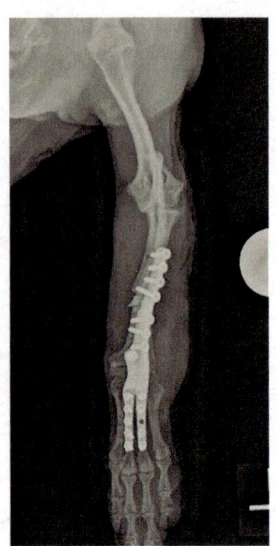

Seeing the photos appeared to make everything more real somehow, and I was shocked at the complexities of the surgery.

I had no idea how I would ever be able to repay this wonderful man for what he had done for my little baby.

Mr. Moores told us that all being well, we could pick up Arlo the following day.

As I put down the phone, I looked out of my window and there, once again, was a little robin standing on the fence in my front garden. I had to smile to myself as I made arrangements to collect Arlo the following day.

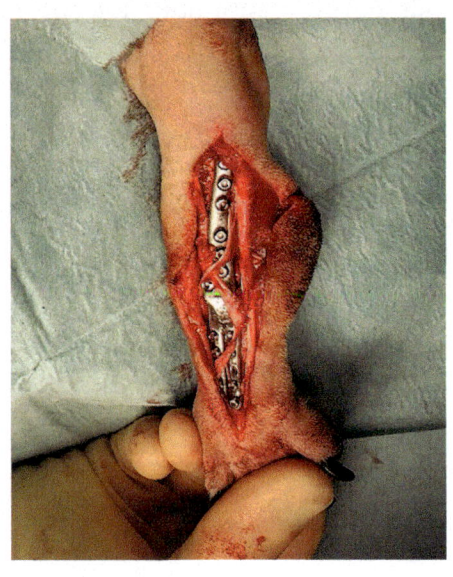

CHAPTER 12

Arlo Now Has One Beautiful Straight Leg

I do not know what I expected to see when I went to pick up Arlo. After looking after him and his two very crooked little legs for the past year, it was very difficult for me to imagine what Arlo would look like with one completely straight leg.

As we pulled up at Anderson Moores I suddenly began to feel apprehensive and very sick. However, as soon as we walked in the door, the staff at the front desk could not have been kinder to us and as we waited to be called into Mr. Moores office, Lyn and I chatted about anything we could think of just to pass the time.

Thinking back, I do not know which one of us was the most anxious about what Arlo was going to look like.

Suddenly the door opened and Mr Moores asked us to come in and sit down while the nurse went to collect Arlo. He explained to us exactly what the surgery had entailed and showed us the latest x-rays of Arlo's leg, now full of metal and looking very straight indeed.

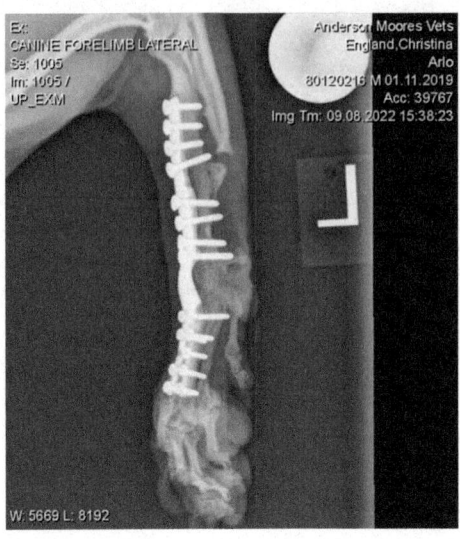

Mr. Moores explained that he had to redesign Arlo's paw because it had been very difficult for him to find enough skin to cover it, after it had been fused. This was because of the damage that Arlo had done to the inside of his forearm, by walking on it for so long.

Suddenly, the door opened and Arlo appeared in the arms of the nurse. As expected, he was extremely pleased to see me and his tail wagged so hard I thought it would fall off. As the nurse handed him to me, I was terrified to even touch him, in case I hurt him but the fear soon melted away once the nurse explained to me exactly how to hold him.

I was surprised to see that his leg only had a little blue bandage on it and not a plaster cast, which I had been expecting. Mr. Moores explained that I needed to cage rest Arlo for six weeks with just gentle lead walks in the garden for him to be able to relieve himself.

He told me to take Arlo to my own vet for a post op check in the next couple of days and have them remove his stitches in ten days' time.

I thanked everyone for everything before Mr. Moores explained to me that Arlo had to begin physiotherapy with their physiotherapist the week after the stitches were removed and asked me to make an appointment at the front desk.

I was very shocked that he was going to begin physiotherapy so soon but he explained that the physiotherapy would help Arlo to begin to use his new leg correctly.

Post Op Check

I made an appointment at Arun Vets a few days later. Arlo was doing extremely well and to everyone's surprise was standing perfectly straight and even trying to stand on his other leg, although of course this was not possible.

The vet passed Arlo with flying colours and we continued to cage rest him for the next ten days while we were waiting for his stitches to heal.

However, when we took Arlo back to have his stitches out, the vet noticed that Arlo's leg was turning black. It was decided that they should call Anderson Moores up for immediate advice, while we waited in the waiting room.

As you can imagine, we were both extremely worried about what this meant for little Arlo. Was he going to lose his leg after everything that we had gone through?

After what appeared to be hours but in reality was around fifteen minutes, the vet appeared holding Arlo in his arms. He explained to us that he had sent the photos off to Andy Moores who had explained that in fact, the leg was doing well and the blackness had been caused by the really large callouses on his legs. He told the vet that he believed that the callouses had been caused by Arlo shuffling along on his forearms. He continued that these had needed to be cut out during his surgery and were now scabbing over.

As you can imagine, we were so relieved to hear that little Arlo was doing well. Our hearts went out to him when we realised just how much pain and suffering he had already endured throughout his short little life.

Of course, Arlo's next adventure would be his first physiotherapy session, at Anderson Moores, the following week.

In the meantime, I continued to keep Arlo on cage rest as instructed but with small walks in the garden to relieve himself.

Little Arlo was improving daily and was really enjoying being able to use his new straighter leg.

Arlo Meets Charly for Physiotherapy

The following week, Helen took us back to Anderson Moores for Arlo's first physiotherapy session with Charly.

We walked Arlo around the outside of the referral unit before we went in, so that Arlo could go to the toilet. This made absolutely no difference whatsoever, because as soon as we sat down and Charly came out to meet us, Arlo decided to go for a poo right in the middle of reception. How embarrassing.

However, this time we came prepared and Helen swiftly cleared up all signs of the poo before we went in.

Charly of course, fell in love with Arlo, despite his little accident. Before the physiotherapy session could begin, she had to whisk Arlo away to be examined. After about ten minutes, she came back all smiles and told us that he was doing brilliantly and we went in to begin his session.

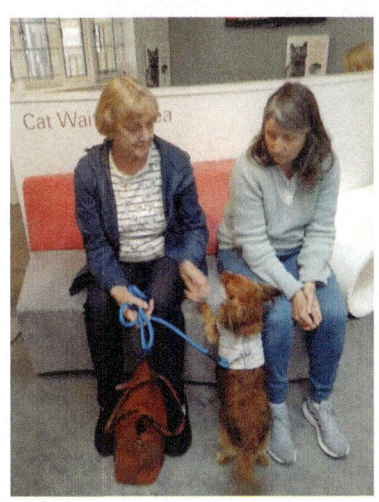

Lyn and Helen with Arlo

After examining just how well Arlo was using his leg, Charly taught us how to do some gentle exercises to strengthen his leg and some massage techniques to help him loosen up his muscles.

The session lasted about 45 minutes and I was given a report card and a program of exercises to do with Arlo on a daily basis.

We carried on seeing Charly, and keeping her up to date with Arlo's progress, for the next few months. Charly was an absolutely wonderful physiotherapist and loved watching his progress nearly as much as we did.

In fact, we found the whole experience very rewarding and cannot praise this referral centre enough for their wonderful expertise and care.

CHAPTER 13

Saying Goodbye and Preparing Arlo for His Second Operation

Just before Christmas 2021, we went to Anderson Moores for our last ever appointment with Andy. Sadly, Mr. Moores had decided

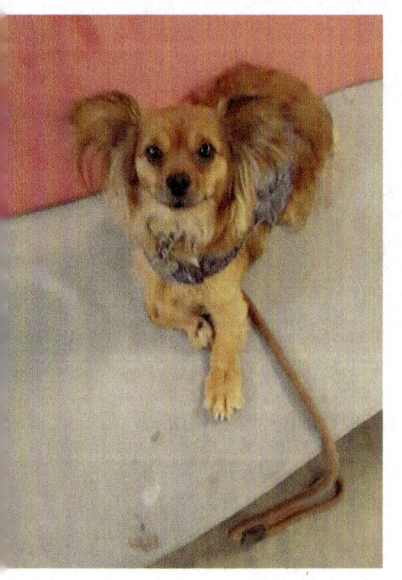

to leave the referral unit and set up his own practice. We were absolutely heartbroken, as over the months we had learned to trust him with our beloved Arlo and the thought of losing him was unbearable.

However, despite our concerns, Mr. Moores assured us that the vet taking over Arlo's case was very experienced and a talented surgeon.

He reassured us that Arlo was doing better than he could have ever hoped for, that Arlo's leg was growing stronger by the day and that he was using it well.

He told me that he believed that much of Arlo's progress was down to my commitment, dedication and the daily physiotherapy routine that I had continued to do with Arlo since his operation.

Mr. Moores continued the appointment by showing us the latest set of x-rays. He explained that Arlo's own bone was beginning to grow onto his plate and that, due to all our hard work, he was beginning to develop strong muscles. He finished the appointment by explaining that although Arlo was doing well he still needed another six weeks of cage rest, before arranging another appointment to hopefully sign him off.

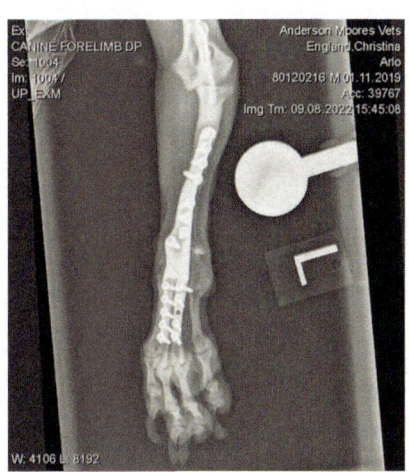

With heavy hearts, we said our goodbyes and wished him all the best for the future.

A New Year A New Beginning

Our last appointment at Anderson Moores, before being introduced to our new surgeon, was in January, 2022.

When we arrived at the referral unit, Arlo was in good spirits. However, once again this did not stop him from doing his usual protest poop in reception. This was despite the fact that we had purposely walked him around the field opposite the clinic before his appointment.

Once the area had been cleaned up, much to our embarrassment, Arlo was taken off for his final set of x-rays.

While we waited, we decided to go to the garden centre with driver Helen, for lunch. We were, of course, very excited because we all knew that Arlo had come such a long way since picking him up as a frightened skinny little dog with wonky front legs, in 2020.

We spent our time chatting about all of Arlo's adventures and reminiscing about just how far we had come in such a short space of time.

A few hours later, we received the call to say that Arlo had had his x-rays and was in recovery.

As soon as we got there, the vet took us into the office to go through the x-ray report and to sign Arlo off. We were told that Arlo did not need any more cage rest and to carry on with his physiotherapy, and to begin hydrotherapy.

I must admit, that I was very relieved at the thought of no more cage rest because Arlo had hated that cage with a vengeance and was always managing to make a bid for freedom, at every opportunity.

Even though I was sleeping downstairs, to be as close to Arlo as possible, somehow Arlo always managed to escape during the night, to sleep with his Mum.

We decided to keep that little piece of information quiet and to this day the vets have never been any the wiser.

The vet explained that we would receive an appointment in a couple of months to be introduced to our new surgeon, Mr. James Grierson.

Although we all felt very excited for Arlo, our excitement was tinged with sadness, as we now realised that we were never going to see Mr. Moores again.

However, our hearts were also filled with optimism for the future.

Arlo Learning to use His New Straight Leg

I think for me, watching Arlo over the next few weeks learning how to use his new straight leg properly, were some of the most memorable times throughout his journey.

Watching him sit, stand and walk tall, was so special.

Watching Arlo take his first steps with a straight leg and a straight back for the first time, was comparable to watching a young toddler getting up onto their feet for the first time. The whole experience was just so amazing and so very special.

Of course, Arlo struggled but to see him with renewed confidence was a fantastic experience, and he was much happier than he had ever been.

CHAPTER 14

Plans for Arlo's Second Leg Begin to Take Shape

Our first meeting with Mr. Grierson took place on 4th March, 2022. I do not know what we expected but what we did not expect was an appointment so quickly after his first leg had been operated on.

When we arrived, we discovered that the centre was still under strict COVID regulations, therefore if we wanted to enter the building we were both asked to wear a mask. Due to suffering from asthma I was not usually required to wear a mask but because I did not know Mr. Grierson and because I felt extremely reluctant to let Arlo be examined without me present, I agreed to wear a mask and comply with the rules on this occasion.

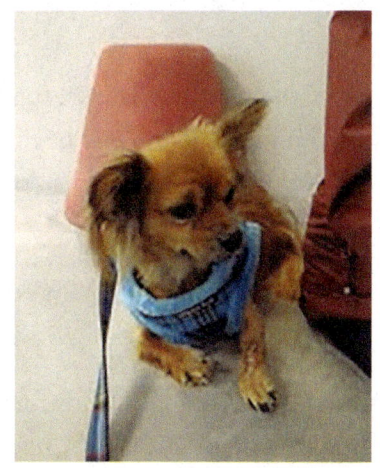

When I went in, Mr. Grierson greeted me with a big smile which immediately put me at ease. He thanked me for wearing a mask and asked if he could have a look at Arlo's legs. He gently put Arlo on the examination table and began to examine his legs in detail. He said that the previous surgery was healing well and that he was pleased to see that Arlo was using the leg well. He then took a range of photos of both legs.

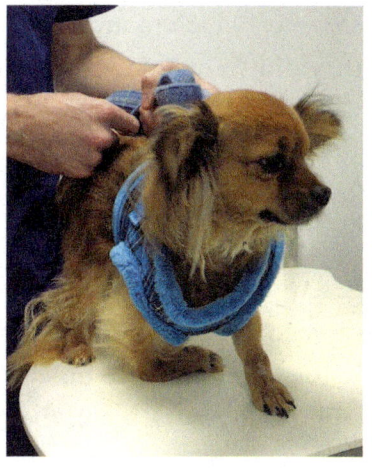

He told me that he believed that he could use Arlo's previous x-rays to guide him and if I was happy to go ahead with the surgery, he would order the cutters and guides.

I agreed that I did want the surgery to go ahead and explained that I would need to do more fundraising to cover the costs.

He said that he wanted to proceed with the surgery in May. I must admit, I was surprised that he wanted to go ahead with Arlo's second leg that soon but agreed with the plans.

More Fundraising and Therapy

Over the next few weeks, fundraising took on a whole new meaning. Funds were by now beginning to dwindle, and if I wanted this surgery to go ahead it was down to me to raise the funds.

I have never worked on anything so hard in all my life as we did trying to raise the funds for Arlo's second operation. Day in and day out, Lyn and I worked solidly raising the funds required.

I tried appealing for funds for Arlo by contacting a variety of celebrities, football clubs and television stations, all to no avail. As a last ditch attempt, I contacted our local newspaper, *The Chichester Observer*, which to my utter surprise contacted me back to say that they did want to do a story on Arlo and not only that but they wanted to feature his story on their front page.

I was stunned, my little Arlo was going to be front page news, well, at least locally.

A few days later, a reporter and a photographer from the Observer came to visit me to discuss Arlo's story in detail. After an interview lasting for about an hour, a range of photographs were taken of Arlo and myself, to feature in their story.

The article was absolutely fantastic and was a huge success. Once again the funds began to roll in. We were so surprised when out of the blue Arlo became somewhat of a local celebrity, with people stopping us in the street for a chat.

On top of all the fundraising, Arlo had begun receiving weekly physiotherapy, with Becky and attending hydrotherapy with the lovely Jane Banatyne, at *121 Animal Therapy*.[10]

I will never forget Arlo's first hydrotherapy lesson because Arlo was not a fan of anything wet. His little face was a picture. First, he had to tolerate a shower and then the hot tub. As it happened, Arlo did enjoy the hot tub, as Jane turned on the warm bubbles, which not only massaged Arlo's legs but also his back, which, by the look on his face, was obviously very soothing. Slowly, this scared little dog began to relax and let the bubbles do their magic. His little face said it all.

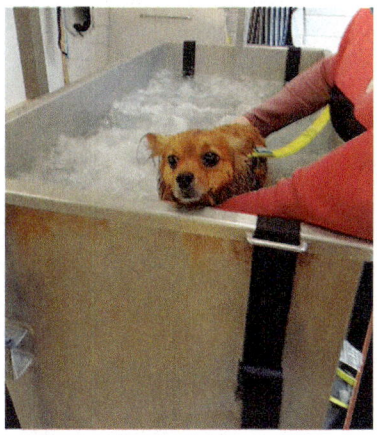
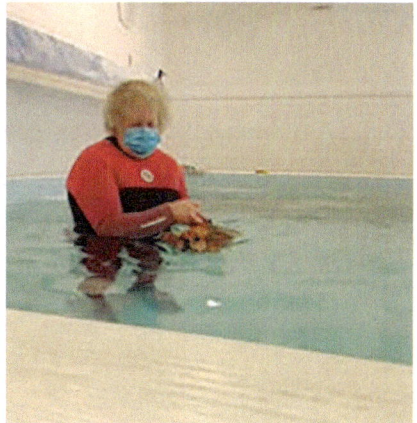

Obviously, it was not all fun and games because Arlo had to do some hard work in the hydrotherapy pool. Although Arlo was not usually a fan of hard work, he embraced his exercises like he did everything else, with grit, determination and a big grin on his face.

It appeared that nothing ever seemed to phase this amazing little dog. However, unbeknown to us, Arlo's biggest challenges lay ahead.

It was not long before I received a telephone call from Anderson Moores with a date for Arlo's surgery, 26th May, 2022.

As I was very keen to show Mr. Grierson Arlo's progress, I emailed him a range of photographs, one of which showed Arlo standing on all four legs, looking as pleased as punch.

Since Arlo's first surgery, Arlo regularly attempted to stand up using all four legs to show us how much he had improved.

These photographs in particular have always been very special to me because they clearly show what a gutsy and determined little dog Arlo was.

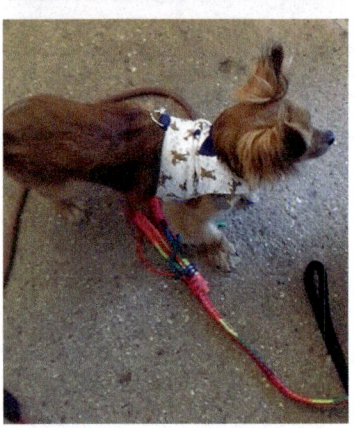

In fact, Arlo would stand straight and upright as often as he could, even though he could only hold the position for a few seconds.

I was so proud of him.

Arlo Standing Tall

CHAPTER 15

Arlo's Second Operation Goes Ahead

It had been decided that Arlo should be admitted to Anderson Moores on 25th May. This was because Mr. Grierson wanted to begin Arlo's surgery as early as possible the following morning.

When we arrived at Anderson Moores, Arlo once again decided to do his signature poo in the middle of the floor. By now, I was so used to this antic that I no longer felt embarrassed. However, today Arlo decided that he would go one step further because as soon as we went into the examination room he decided to show his appreciation by throwing up all over poor Mr. Grierson's shoes.

However, Mr. Grierson took it all in his stride and after he had cleared up the mess, he began to examine little Arlo. I asked him if he felt nervous about the surgery, and he said that he didn't feel nervous at all because he was well prepared and had Arlo's previous x-rays and scans to guide him.

Mr. Grierson continued by explaining the procedure to us and out-lined all the possible risks. He said that we would have to make sure that Arlo remained on strict cage rest after his operation because his bones were exceptionally fragile. He explained that if he should suffer a fracture after the surgery because of the nature of his disabilities, he would either require an amputation or he would need to be put to sleep. Shocked, I told him that there was absolutely no way that I was going to even consider having Arlo put down and that I would do everything I could to keep him safe.

After the consultation, I gave Arlo a big hug and told him that he was going to be just fine. Mr. Grierson proceeded by giving Arlo to the nurse, as we said our goodbyes. However, before we went, we asked Mr. Grierson if we could take a photograph of him holding Arlo.

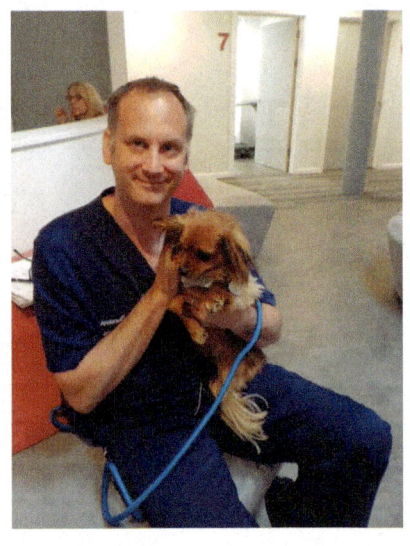

Mr. Grierson then told us that the next time we would see Arlo he would be standing up on all four legs.

Somehow, it was hard to imagine him upright on all four legs but I knew in my heart that I was doing the best that I could for my wonky little boy.

As I left, like before, I felt an enormous wave of sadness because I knew that I was about to lose those crooked little legs forever and I could not help wondering if, by losing his crooked little legs he would still be the mischievous, cheeky little Arlo that I become to love so much.

I can honestly say that all day long on the 26th May, I was a bag of nerves. I was extremely worried about whether or not everything would go to plan and whether Arlo would be able to survive another operation so soon after the previous surgery.

I needn't have worried because at around 3pm, Mr. Grierson phoned to say that everything had gone to plan and my little Arlo was in recovery. He told me that despite the fact that Arlo had very tiny, fragile bones, the operation had gone extremely well and that Arlo now had two straight front legs for the first time in his life.

He explained that they wanted to keep Arlo in overnight but we could come and pick him up the following day. I cannot even begin to explain just how relieved I was and how much I was looking forward to picking him up.

Even though I knew Arlo was safe and that he had come through the surgery, I still felt really scared about picking him up and how I was going to manage to look after him during his recovery. It is one thing to decide to foster a little dog like Arlo but another one entirely putting yourself through the emotional rollercoaster that comes with looking after a dog that was as disabled as he was.

I don't think that anyone could have ever prepared me for the emotions that I experienced that night, as I tried to mentally prepare myself to collect Arlo the following day, and as we approached Anderson Moores, I don't think either Lyn or myself knew quite what to expect.

When we got there, we were greeted with the same friendly welcome that we always got from the amazing team of receptionists.

Despite their warm welcome, I do not think I have ever felt as nervous as I did that day. My legs felt like jelly, as Mr. Grierson called us into the consultation room. However, I needn't have worried because as usual he was very kind and understanding. He said that Arlo was

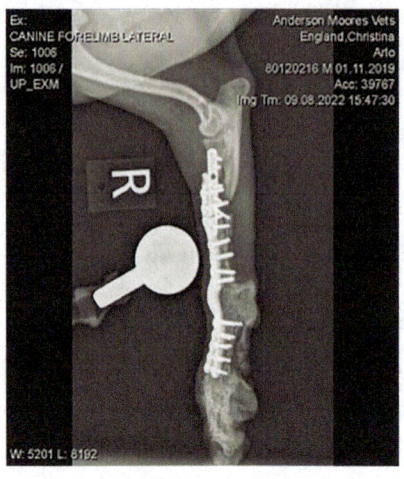

a lovely little dog and explained to me that the operation had gone to plan and that Arlo was doing really well. He showed us both his x-rays and explained exactly what he had done to correct Arlo's deformities.

It's a good job I have a strong stomach because the details of his operation were quite graphic.

Mr. Grierson explained to us that Arlo had to be kept on strict cage rest for the next six weeks, with absolutely no walking, running or jumping. He said that Arlo could only be taken into the garden on a lead to go to the toilet.

He asked me how Arlo was going to travel home and I told him that Arlo had a special crate which I then gave to him.

Mr. Grierson handed the crate to the nurse and asked us to wait outside while she went to fetch Arlo.

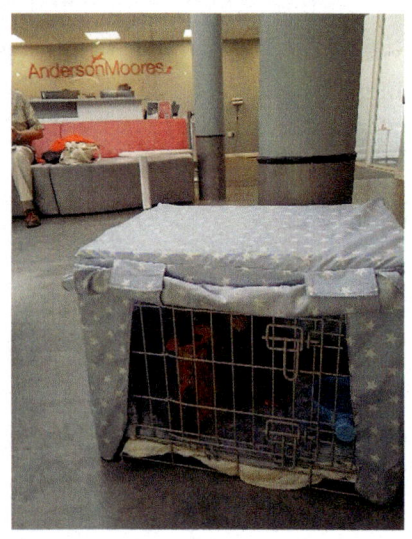

I didn't know what to expect as the nurse returned with Arlo but I didn't expect Arlo to come home with just a bandage on his now beautifully straight leg. The moment I saw him, I burst into tears. As I looked down at his little straight legs for the first time, I felt all my fears and concerns just melt away and relief flood my body. He looked so tiny and vulnerable and so excited to see me. His little tail wagged and wagged, as he tried to stand up on his little straight legs for the first time in his life and as he did, he gently kissed my hand through the cage door.

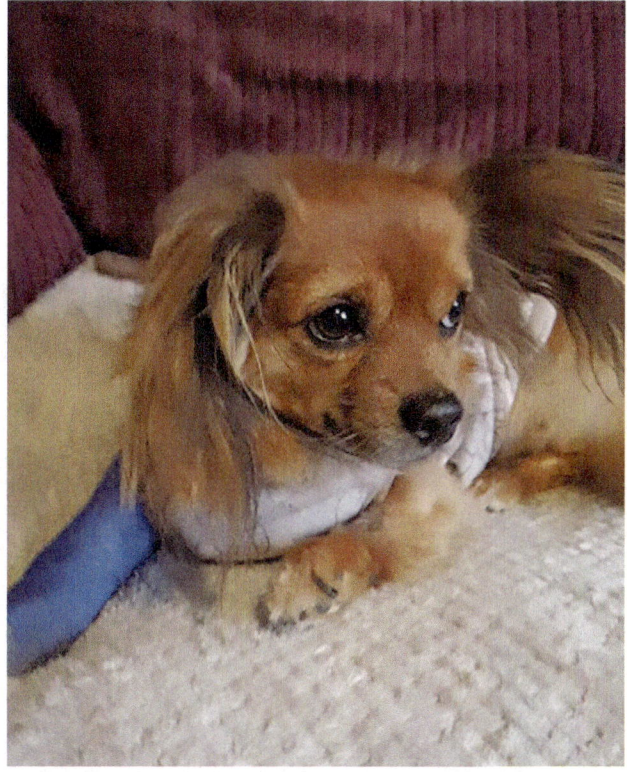

At that moment, I felt such an enormous rush of love for this amazing little dog and I vowed that whatever happened to him in the future, I would love him and care for him for the rest of his life.

CHAPTER 16

Sadly, Our Happiness was Short Lived

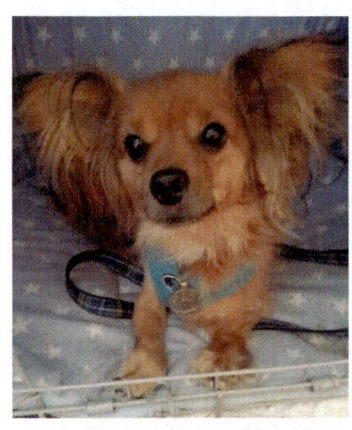

For the first few days, Arlo came on in leaps and bounds. He began to regularly stand up, tall and upright and could even walk a little on lead in the garden. However, when we returned to Storrington, for Arlo's wound to be checked, it was very clear that he had an infection. We were absolutely devastated because he had been doing so well. He was immediately put on antibiotics and ten days later he returned to Storrington to have his leg checked and to have his stitches removed.

Over the next few weeks, Arlo improved beyond all expectations and I slowly became a little more confident and began to allow Arlo to walk on his own in the garden, while I walked behind him supervising his every move.

I did this because Arlo was not great at walking on his lead and I did not want to pull him, in case I damaged his leg. He was doing so well that I can honestly say 1 was not worried in the slightest. However, with hindsight maybe I should have been a lot more worried than I was.

I was so proud of him and got Lyn to take loads of photographs and videos of him taking his first steps.

He continued to do well and at the time we thought that everything was going to go like clockwork, like it had done previously. However, on June 6th, just a few weeks before his check up at Anderson Moores, I was giving him a cuddle in his cage, when he suddenly leapt out and ran across the floor to Lyn and as he did so he let out this blood curdling scream. Suddenly, everything appeared to stop still. I raced over to Arlo and picked him up and tried to soothe him but he was not having any of it and just continued to scream. I will never ever forget that scream, it was ear piercing and appeared to go forever and in that moment, I knew in my heart that Arlo had broken his leg.

I raced him over to Storrington, but I knew without him even being examined or having the x-rays, that Arlo's leg was broken. As I waited for the results, Mr. Grierson's words echoed in my ears. I kept asking myself, if it was my fault, or if I had done something wrong? I was convinced that I had caused Arlo's injury. It was all my fault that he had hurt his leg, I should never have tried to help him and agree to surgery. I went over and over everything in my head. Should he have walked off lead, even with me a few paces behind him? Should he have ever come out of the cage in the first place?

Suddenly, the vet appeared carrying Arlo in his arms. One look at his face confirmed my worst fears. Arlo had broken his leg right at the top of his plate.

I was told to cage rest Arlo until I could get an appointment with Anderson Moores.

Sadly, I was not able to get an appointment for a few weeks and when I did, Mr. Grierson confirmed that Arlo had indeed broken his leg and that sadly, the operation had failed.

However, instead of recommending an amputation as I had expected, Mr. Grierson suggested performing a second surgery. He explained that it might just be possible to put in a second very small plate above the first one, in the hope that this would strengthen Arlo's leg and encourage the bone to grow onto the plate.

Although I was extremely worried about whether Arlo would be able to cope with yet another operation, I agreed, in the hope that Mr. Grierson would be able to save his leg.

It was agreed that Arlo's second operation would take place on June 29th, 2022.

CHAPTER 17

More Sadness as Arlo's Leg Breaks Again

To begin with, Arlo's second operation to attach another plate into the top of Arlo's leg, was a huge success. Once again Arlo was coming on in leaps and bounds. However, sadly our optimism that everything was going to work out this time was short lived, as no

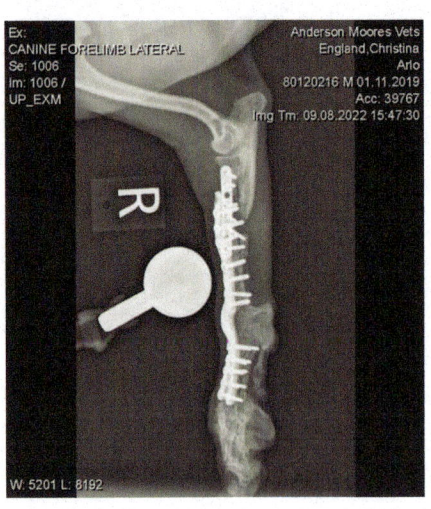

matter how hard I tried to do everything one hundred percent correctly, it appeared that Arlo had other ideas.

For the first few weeks everything appeared to be going extremely well, but, one night after we came back from a fundraising event, Arlo got so excited to see us all that he shot his little arm through the bars of the cage.

It was like deja vue, because suddenly, Arlo let out this blood curdling scream and as we all looked at one another, I think we all knew instantly that Arlo had once again fractured his leg.

I went over to his crate and gently lifted him out and put him on the floor. However, to my surprise he began to walk. In my naivety, at that moment I truly believed that maybe, just maybe he was going to be alright.

Over the next few days, I hardly let him move. I even went out and bought a canvas crate. I tried so hard to be positive but deep down I think I always knew that I was just kidding myself and that his little leg was broken and it was for that reason that I decided to take him back to the vets.

After taking an x-ray my vet confirmed that Arlo's leg was indeed broken and he made arrangements for me to take him back to Anderson Moores.

When I did take Arlo back, Mr. Grierson explained to me that Arlo had developed what was known as a *non-union fracture*. This means that no matter how hard you try, the fracture site simply refuses to knit together.[11]

He said the only answer was to either have Arlo's leg amputated or to end his suffering completely and put him to sleep.

As Arlo was only fostered, I had been regularly speaking about his progress to Hessa at *Hessa's Homeless Hounds*. She had been extremely supportive and had had several lengthy conversations with not only Anderson Moores but with my own vet at Arun Veterinary Group.

Like myself, she wanted everything that could be done for Arlo to be done and we both agreed that putting him to sleep was never going to be an option.

Both Hessa and myself had always known that fixing Arlo's legs could be problematic, and throughout the entire process, I had been discussing alternative treatments with her. She had always agreed with me, that should his surgery fail, that we should try alternative treatments.

As I am and always have been a great believer in natural remedies, I begged Mr. Grierson to let me try to heal Arlo's leg naturally. I asked him if I could take him home and for the next six weeks treat him naturally, with homeopathy and other alternative remedies. I told him that if these treatments did not work and Arlo's leg still refused to heal, I would take him to my own vet for an amputation.

I explained to him that if Arlo did eventually need his leg to be amputated, there were other alternatives, to help him walk on four legs.

I told him that I had always known that Arlo's surgery could fail and that he may need an amputation and it was for this reason that I had been looking into non-surgical prosthetics. I showed him photos of various dogs that had been using these types of prosthetics extremely successfully.[8] Mr. Grierson was not convinced that these types of prosthetics would be able to help Arlo, due to his size. However, he told me that there was no harm in looking at alternative solutions to help Arlo.

Although Mr. Grierson agreed for me to take Arlo home and try to heal the leg naturally, he did make it very clear to me that in his professional opinion there were no remedies that he knew of that could possibly help to heal a non-union fracture.

Deep down, I always knew that he was right; however, I knew that it was my duty as Arlo's carer to do absolutely everything in my power to give him every chance possible.

I explained to Mr. Grierson that while I respected his opinion, I believed that there was no harm in trying every avenue possible.

I thanked him for everything that he had tried to do for Arlo. I knew that although his surgery had failed, Mr. Grierson had done everything in his power to help him and I could see from his x-rays that his skill in performing the intricate surgery was second to none.

Mr. Grierson then took Arlo into the treatment area to put a cast on his broken leg. When he returned, Lyn and I thanked him and all the staff for everything that they had done for Arlo and said our goodbyes.

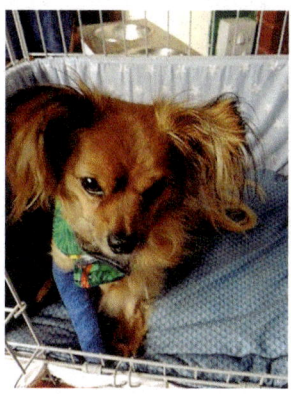 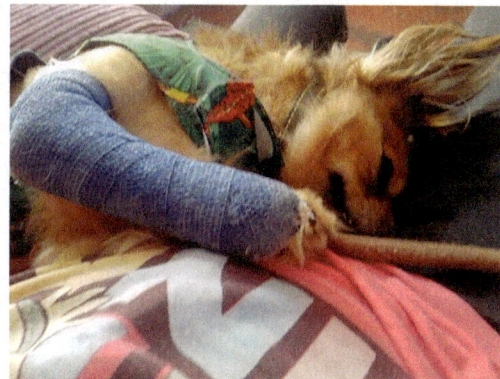

Six Long Weeks Working With a Homeopath

When we got home, I once again put my poor little Arlo into his cage, to begin yet more cage rest and began to search for a reputable homeopath online.

Before my search began, I decided to explain what had happened to Arlo's followers on his social media page. Then I joined as many online groups as I could for using natural remedies for dogs.

Amazingly, within just a few hours of me posting Arlo's story, a homeopath who I already knew, Kate Birch, messaged me on Facebook to say that she was willing to try to help Arlo.

I knew that Ms. Birch was a leading homeopath who lectured all over the world on the amazing powers of homeopathy and that she usually works with humans. I can honestly say that I was in complete shock to think that she would even consider giving up her valuable time to try to help Arlo

Of course, as with all procedures, pharmaceutical products and natural remedies, there are no guarantees. Homeopathy is not a miracle cure but in some cases, by using the remedies correctly, it can completely heal the most complex of medical problems.

After I explained to her Arlo's story in detail, we discussed all the remedies that might be able to help Arlo. I was willing to try anything that I possibly could, while still using his prescription medication.

Over the next six long weeks, I worked daily alongside this wonderful lady.

The remedies we used to try to help little Arlo were:

- Silica
- Arnica
- Conium Mac
- Calcarea Phosphorica
- Carc

I can honestly say that during the time I was using homeopathic remedies for Arlo, his health did improve, the texture and quality of his fur improved, he appeared to have more energy and looked one hundred percent better than he had done previously.

It was soon time for me to take him back to my own vets to see if the leg was healing or if all our hard work had been in vain.

The day I took him back to Arun vets, I felt sick with worry. However, to my amazement, after x-raying him, my vet came back into the room with a very large smile on his face and told me that according to the x-rays, he believed that Arlo's leg was beginning to heal.

My vet then brought Arlo into the waiting room in a brand new splint, where I gave him a really long hug before placing him into his carry case to go home.

He told me that as Arlo appeared to be doing so well, I should continue with what I was doing and bring him back in another six weeks.

I went away that day, feeling absolutely wonderful. On the way home, I treated Arlo to a new toy to keep his mind occupied while he was continuing to heal. I bought him a toy that I could hide treats in. He absolutely loved it and still plays with it today.

We continued to work with the homeopath for another six weeks. However, when I went back to my vet on 30th August, 2022, for a further x-ray, my vet confirmed that sadly, Arlo's leg had broken once again. Reluctantly and with great sadness I knew that I just could not leave it any longer, it wasn't fair on Arlo and with a heavy heart I decided to make an appointment for Arlo to have his leg amputated. This was the last thing that I had ever wanted to do but I knew in my heart that I could not put Arlo through any more trauma or pain.

I booked the appointment for Arlo's amputation for 9th September, 2022

CHAPTER 18

Change of Plan and Renewed Hope

Even with a large splint on it, Arlo's little leg looked so straight, and so perfect, it was heart-breaking to know that in just a few short weeks, it would need to be amputated.

As the days went by, I began to question every single decision that I had ever made.

I asked myself whether or not I should have left him with his crooked legs? Could he have coped with just physiotherapy and hydrotherapy and was it my fault that things had gone so terribly wrong?

One thing was for certain, I knew that he would never cope with three legs because he had so many other complex disabilities.

As I muddled through those dark days, doing everything I could to help Arlo to stay safe and happy, I was filled with guilt and sadness.

However, one evening just before Arlo was due to have his leg amputated, the phone rang. It was my vet. He asked me whether or not I definitely wanted Arlo's leg amputated, if there was any possibility of saving it. I said no, of course not.

He continued by telling me about another little dog that had had similar problems to Arlo. He explained that in this particular case, the vet involved had used a special type of splint, called a spica splint.

He explained that spica splints are often used to completely immobilise a limb, particularly if the dog had injured its shoulder or its elbow.

He said that he believed this type of splint might be able to help Arlo. However, it was extremely heavy, and would need to go right across Arlo's back and damaged shoulder. He said that these kinds of splints were usually used on larger breeds; however, even though there were no guarantees, in his opinion it was worth a go.

I was completely taken aback and told him that if he really thought that it might be able to save Arlo's leg, then of course I would be willing to try anything.

So on the 9th September, 2022, instead of taking my little Arlo for his planned amputation, I took him to be fitted with his first spica splint, instead.

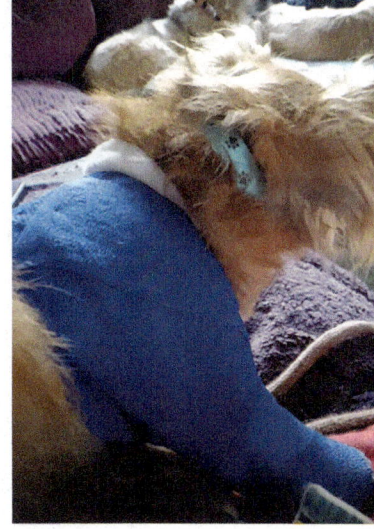

I must admit, when I went back to the vets that day to pick him up, my eyes filled up with tears as he walked out of the treatment area, as proud as punch in his beautiful bright blue spica splint.

Although my vet said that Arlo was still to be kept safe and prevented from doing any running and jumping, with a spica splint he was now allowed to go for small lead walks instead of being confined to complete cage rest. He was also prescribed weekly physiotherapy to help keep his remaining limbs strong.

Over the next few weeks, Arlo appeared to be doing well. Because he could only wear his splint for up to six weeks at a time, he was soon due for his splint to be changed.

It was decided that Arlo should have his first splint change at the beginning of October and when the time came for me to take Arlo for his next appointment I was really worried about the outcome. Gut feeling, I suppose.

Letting Arlo go was always difficult, but this time was one of the most difficult times ever. You see, while Arlo had the spica splint on, whatever was going underneath, I could kid myself that everything was absolutely fine and that Arlo was just like any other little dog.

He was able to walk on his lead and although he wore a little boot to protect the end of the splint, he not only looked so well and so happy, he looked much the same as any other little dog.

However, once I had booked him in and signed the forms for Arlo to have an anaesthetic, I knew that in reality, the vet could phone me and tell me that it hadn't worked and Arlo needed to have an amputation.

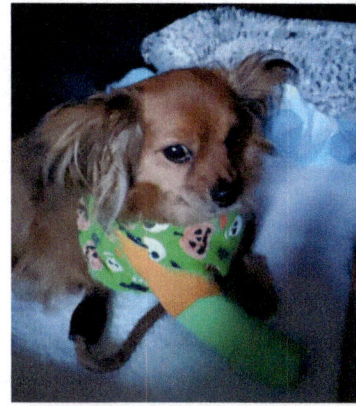

To take my mind off the whole situation, I decided to spend the day fundraising. This was because if my vet did decide to give Arlo a further spica splint, it could cost me over £300. With that and Arlo's weekly physiotherapy sessions, his remaining veterinary costs and all of his homeopathic and natural remedies, this little foster dog was costing me well over £600 a month.

At around 2 pm, my vet phoned and he sounded really positive.

He told me that I was not to get my hopes up too much but in his opinion Arlo's leg had improved and that he had decided to put a new spica splint on and when I was ready, I could come and pick him up.

When I arrived, Arlo came out of the treatment area boasting a rather special Halloween themed spica splint. We had to laugh because the whole team had made such an effort and Arlo looked absolutely fantastic. I do not think I will ever be able to thank them enough because after all the turmoil of the last year, it really did cheer me up.

I had even brought along a new Halloween harness to keep Arlo warm on his journey home. He looked absolutely spectacular that day and I was so proud.

As I had now been fostering Arlo for a total of two years, I decided that on November 28th, which was exactly two years after I had begun fostering Arlo, I would make it official. I had now cared for Arlo for nearly two years and I knew that I loved him too much to ever let him be adopted by another family. It was for this reason that I had finally decided to adopt Arlo and become his forever Mummy.

Of course I had to finalise everything with Hessa but when I phoned her to ask, she was extremely happy that I had decided to adopt Arlo and agreed to send me the papers to sign.

To make the day even more special, I got a friend of mine to make Arlo a very special harness declaring him adopted.

CHAPTER 19

Hoping and Praying for a Christmas Miracle

It had been decided that Arlo should have his next splint change in the middle of December, with a check-up in between. However, on Arlo's check-up, we found out that his leg had developed a pressure sore, so it was necessary to have an earlier than planned splint change.

My vet decided that Arlo should have another set of x-rays to see how his leg was doing and some antibiotics to heal his pressure sore.

Sadly, the x-rays revealed that Arlo's leg had deteriorated. However, instead of an amputation as I had expected, it was decided that as he still had a blood supply, albeit a weak one, supplying the leg, that instead of an amputation, Arlo should be fitted with one last spica splint.

If, however, this splint failed to heal Arlo's leg, then we all felt that it would be unfair to put Arlo through any more traumas and his leg would be amputated.

When I collected Arlo later that day, he came out wearing a beautiful Christmas themed spica splint. He looked so sweet and as soon as we got home, we took some photos.

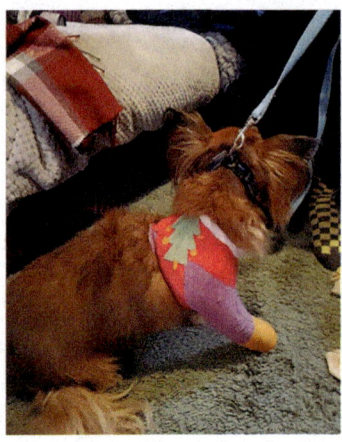 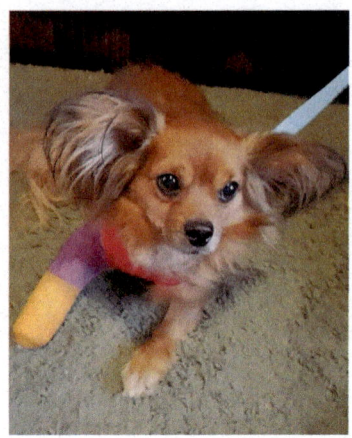

With Arlo's new splint, came hope of a Christmas Miracle but sadly, a miracle for Arlo was not on the cards that year because even though we were trying to keep Arlo safe during this period and continuing with his physiotherapy as instructed, it appears as if lady luck was not on our side.

Disaster as Arlo Develops a Really Nasty Infection

I am unsure exactly how we got through that Christmas because late on Christmas Eve, it was clear to me that Arlo had developed a really nasty infection, not in his bad leg but in his good leg.

His leg appeared to be turning black and was extremely smelly, with pus coming out from underneath the top of his splint.

As soon as I discovered the problem, I phoned the veterinary hospital who told me to bring him in straight away. However, as I do not drive and had no way of getting him there, after sending the vet some photos of the infection, it was decided that as they were so busy I should go to one of their smaller branches by taxi and pick up some antibiotics.

Despite the fact that at Christmastime taxis were double the price, I decided that I was not taking any chances and raced over to Chichester to collect the medication.

The next day, which was Christmas Day, my own vet phoned me from his home and told me to take Arlo into their Chichester branch the following day and they would change his splint that was obviously so tight that it was beginning to dig into the top of his good leg.

Even though it was Boxing Day, Mr Derek Spooner, who ran the pet ambulance service, took me to Chichester, to get Arlo's splint changed. It was decided that, to give the infection a chance to heal, Arlo should be fitted with a normal splint for around a week.

The following week, when my own vet eventually got to see Arlo, he decided that Arlo should be fitted with a further slightly looser spica splint to make sure that Arlo's infection and pressure sore were completely healed before taking any further x-rays.

When he gave Arlo back to me that day, he apologised, and told me, with a twinkle in his eye, that the girls had accidentally put a bright pink splint on Arlo.

We did laugh, when we saw poor Arlo with his bright pink leg. He was so embarrassed that catching a photo with him in the pink splint was not easy.

My vet had also decided to dress Arlo's wound with a Manuka honey dressing and he told me that I could use Manuka honey on the pressure sore to aid recovery.[10]

He explained to me that Manuka honey was a natural antibiotic and he believed that it would really help Arlo. He told me that I could also use a syringe to put Manuka honey down his splint.

Although I completely trusted his views and opinions, I was surprised that he wanted me to syringe Manuka honey into his splint because all I could picture was Arlo and I becoming extremely sticky in the process

However, once home, I decided that as Arlo loved honey, I would also give him a teaspoon of manuka honey every day, which I have to admit Arlo thoroughly enjoyed.

CHAPTER 20

A Sticky Mess and a New Spica Splint

Getting manuka honey inside the splint was not easy. Within a few days, everything became sticky and covered in honey. The honey made all of Arlo's covers and bedding sticky and I spent the next couple of weeks changing his bedding daily and making sure that Arlo's wound was kept as clean and sterile as possible.

I found this very frustrating and time consuming. Arlo, on the other hand, thought that it was great fun and spent hours licking the honey off his splint.

After I had been treating Arlo's pressure sore and his fractured leg with the manuka honey for around two and a half weeks, it was time to head back to the vets.

When my vet saw the state of Arlo, he did laugh as he proceeded to clear up all the honey. The good news was that the treatment had worked and his pressure sore had completely healed. My vet was so pleased with Arlo's progress that he decided to put one final new spica splint onto his leg. This was because due to him developing a pressure sore, Arlo had only managed to keep the Christmas themed splint on for a few weeks.

The good thing about the change of splint was the fact that Arlo no longer had to go around wearing his Barbie pink splint and came out wearing a green one.

My vet explained that if Arlo's leg showed absolutely no sign of healing over the next six weeks, it would mean that the leg was no longer viable and that he would need an amputation.

At this stage, as heart-breaking as this decision would be for all of us, I knew that he was right and that an amputation may be the kindest thing that I could do for Arlo if this spica splint failed to improve his leg.

Sadly, over time, I had noticed that the spark had begun to fade in Arlo's eyes. He looked as if his little body was giving up and that he had very little fight left in him.

This had been such a tough journey for little Arlo. He only weighed 6 kilos and he had been the bravest little dog ever but as difficult as this decision would be, I could see that his little body could not take a lot more.

On a more positive note, over the past four months, I had been regularly in touch with an American company called *3D Pets Prosthetics*.[11] 3DPets is the sister company to DiveDesign and they make non-surgical prosthetics using 3D printing for front leg amputee dogs.

I had already discussed Arlo's story with them and they believed that, if Arlo did need to have his leg amputated, he would be a suitable candidate for one of their prosthetics.

Although, of course I had always wanted Arlo to be able to keep his legs and be just like any other little dog, I had always known that surgeons cannot perform miracles and that although both Mr. Grierson and Mr. Moores' surgeries were first class and that they had both done their absolute best for Arlo, I knew realistically that there was always a risk of the surgeries failing.

I decided that as an amputation was now becoming a real possibility, I would begin to take Arlo out for gentle walks. This was because I wanted more than anything in the world, for Arlo to be a normal little dog again.

He had spent the last couple of months on cage rest and I could see that he was desperate to go out and about with the others. The vet had always smiled at Arlo because he used his splint as a peg leg, so I knew that Arlo could walk well for short distances.

From the very first spica splint, the vets had always me that the splint needed to be protected and that he needed to wear a little boot, I had bought Arlo a little silver boot and whenever, I had taken him out in his stroller or out into garden he had always worn his silver boot.

As it was important for Arlo to be kept safe at all times, I used to put him in his stroller and walk the other smaller dogs alongside.

These walks were what we called, *'Arlo's Special Times,'* and we always took them to the park, or the woods, or the country lanes then took Arlo out of his stroller and let him have a good old sniff and a little walk around.

I cannot even begin to tell you how much he enjoyed these times and we took hundreds of photos to keep as memories.

Tough Decisions Required

Arlo was booked in to have his final spica splint removed on 24th February, 2023.

As the day arrived, my head was all over the place. I felt sick with worry. I think that I had already made my decision and knew deep down that I was never going to see Arlo on four legs again.

As I handed him to the nurse, I just couldn't help shedding a tear. I told the nurse that unless they could see a significant difference, I wanted Arlo to have his leg removed.

I knew that it was no longer fair on Arlo to put him through any more and I could see that Arlo had enough.

The nurse promised me that they would take extra special care of him and assured me that if an amputation was required, then Arlo would walk out of the vets as if nothing had happened.

Deep down I doubted that but her words were comforting nevertheless.

Later that afternoon, I received the phone call that I had been dreading. My vet explained that sadly, the blood supply to Arlo's leg had begun to die and that his little leg was now, for the first time, turning black. I asked him if there was anything else that he could do to save his leg.

He said that, sadly, there were no other options left and that he believed that the kindest and most ethical thing that we could all do for Arlo now, was an amputation.

I reluctantly agreed as I did not want to see Arlo suffer.

A few hours later, my vet phoned to tell me that Arlo had now had his amputation and that he was in recovery and doing well. He told me that the operation had gone well and Arlo could come home later that day.

When Lyn and I went to the vets to collect Arlo, we could not believe it when little Arlo came running out to the waiting room on three legs.

As usual he was very pleased to see his Mum and ran up to me with his tail wagging. I must admit, I was extremely pleased to see him looking so well and happy, although it was very difficult for me to come to terms with the fact that Arlo's beautiful little leg that we had all tried to save, had now been tossed into the incinerator like rubbish.

I asked Lyn if she would hold him while I took the very first photo of Arlo with three legs.

CHAPTER 21

Arlo's New Beginning

As expected, life on three legs was not easy for Arlo, especially in the early days. Unlike many dogs, who embraced their new life without pain, Arlo found adapting to his new life really difficult.

First, he just couldn't get used to wearing his little body suit, which he was given to prevent him from licking his wound. It got in his way when he tried to pass urine and I had to buy him two more, just to keep him clean, dry and smelling a little sweeter.

One of his biggest challenges for Arlo after his amputation was going to the toilet. To pass urine, Arlo had always stood on his front right leg and cock his back left leg. Without his front right leg, not only did he continually fall on his nose, which he still does today, but he repeatedly fell on his amputation site, which made healing even more difficult.

I tried using a sling as recommended, to enable Arlo to stand and walk in a more upright position but I found this incredibly difficult because of Arlo's size.

Another problem that we encountered was that in Arlo's head he still

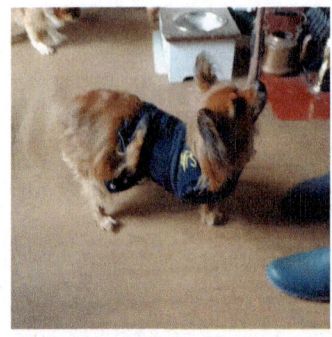

had his missing limb, causing him to continually scream out in pain.

Concerned that he was in pain, I took him to the vets but they could find no problem. The amputation site was clean and was healing well. However, they did explain to me that like humans, some dogs suffer from, '*Phantom Limb Syndrome*,'[12] after an amputation.

Poor Arlo, he had been through so much and although he was now up and about, life on three limbs was proving to be a struggle.

Ten days after his amputation, Arlo had his stitches out and after a couple of follow up appointments, the vet told me that I was to take Arlo away and treat him like any other normal little dog.

Of course, with a dog like Arlo, treating him like a normal little dog was far from easy. This is because Arlo is and has always been the biggest drama queen going.

In the early days, every time Arlo had screamed because he had hurt himself, we had always rushed over to see if he was alright and showered him with love and cuddles.

Big mistake, because by doing this, we had inadvertently taught Arlo that by screaming he would get what he wanted.

Not only did Arlo scream when he accidentally got knocked or when any of the vets approached him to do even the most simple of procedures but Arlo would now scream to get whatever his little heart desired.

Of course, breaking him of this habit has been exceptionally difficult because whenever Arlo wanted anything, he would just scream and scream at the top of his voice until he got it.

One of our biggest problems has always been when we have had visitors. While all of the others would bark, like normal dogs, Arlo would just continue to scream at the top of his voice. Of course this continual screaming always got their attention and he would always get fussed over first.

Although we have continued to work hard on Arlo's behaviour and his screaming for attention has improved, unfortunately, it is, and always has been, extremely difficult to ignore an exceptionally cute dog, doing a Meer cat impression, while screaming at the top of his voice.

As I explained earlier, life on three legs was extremely difficult for Arlo. Although, in many ways, he had improved and was no longer in pain, because his left leg was full of metal and his ankle had been fused, it meant that Arlo had to put the majority of his weight on a weak front leg, which for him was near on impossible.

The continual strain that Arlo was now putting on his remaining front leg, was causing Arlo's elbow to collapse under him.

We really did try and I must admit taking him onto the beach again without worrying was a breath of fresh air. Although he thoroughly enjoyed his first outing on the beach since his amputation, he

really did struggle and I decided that to make his life easier Arlo definitely needed a prosthetic leg.

As it had been three or four weeks since his amputation I decided to get in touch with 3DPets[13] and enquire about which was the best type of prosthetic for him.

I filled in the online form and explained his story. I sent them loads of photos and videos and they told me that they could definitely help Arlo.

The only problem that I could see was the fact that we were in the UK and they were in the US.

However, they reassured me that this was not a problem because they had already helped around fifteen dogs in the UK. They explained to me that, if I agreed to go ahead, they would be one hundred percent committed to helping Arlo.

I was absolutely ecstatic because the photos and videos that I had seen of other dogs using their prosthetics online were absolutely mind blowing.

Unlike surgical prosthetics, where dogs are required to have their prosthetics surgically attached which can sometimes lead to infection and failure, non-surgical prosthetics can be simply strapped to the dog, using a type of harness or cage that the dog sits in, which is then strapped onto the dog using Velcro.

Here are a few photos of another dog, Tripp, wearing a prosthetic made by 3DPets, which I was given by his owner Lydia Mindek, to use in Arlo's book.

As I definitely wanted to go ahead with one of their prosthetics for Arlo, I arranged a telephone consultation with one of their technicians.

The telephone call was arranged for 16th March, 2023.

After a few teething problems with my computer, I managed to speak to Alex, the managing director of 3DPets.

Alex explained that to make Arlo a prosthetic, they would need to send me a casting kit, to make a plaster cast of Arlo's body. He explained that this would enable them to make Arlo a harness that would fit perfectly to the shape of his body. Alex said that they also required a range of photographs of Arlo standing in different positions and a full set of his measurements.

The very thought of me trying to get Arlo to stand still, while I put a body stocking on him and then the plaster, filled me with absolute horror.

I told Alex that this all sounded extremely complicated and I was unsure that I would be able to get Arlo to cooperate. However, Alex reassured me and told me not to worry because in many cases vets can do this for the owner.

As I knew that my vet was one hundred percent on board with my decision to get a prosthetic leg for Arlo, I told him that I was sure that my vet would be able to help me to do the cast, as well as take the photographs and all the measurements that were required.

Alex told me that I would receive the kit by the end of the month.

I thanked him and we said goodbye.

CHAPTER 22

Excitement as Arlo's Casting Kit Arrives

Arlo's casting kit arrived on 26th March, 2023. I cannot begin to explain how excited we were because Lyn and I both knew that this kit was going to be the beginning of a completely new chapter in Arlo's life.

All the pain and heartache of the past year was finally behind us and we both knew that this simple little kit was going to really enable Arlo to have the life on four legs that we had always dreamed of.

As expected, the kit looked very complicated and as I cannot even put the simplest of flat packs together, I knew that there was no way that I could attempt to make a cast of Arlo's body that would even begin to resemble Arlo.

I decided that I would definitely need to ask my vet to assist. However, even the vet had reservations and decided that it would be in everyone's best interest to give Arlo a light anaesthetic before attempting the procedure.

As the next available date for Arlo to be admitted was 19th April, 2023, we decided to definitely go ahead on that date.

What Happened Next Surprised Us All

On the day that Arlo was due to have the cast of his body made, Arlo decided to surprise everyone by completely cooperating with the team, throughout the procedure. It was as if he knew what we were trying to do for him.

When my vet phoned me to go and pick Arlo up, he told me that Arlo had not needed an anaesthetic and had in fact been the perfect model. Not only had he stood perfectly still for the photographs and his measurements to be taken but had even stood still while the plaster cast was drying.

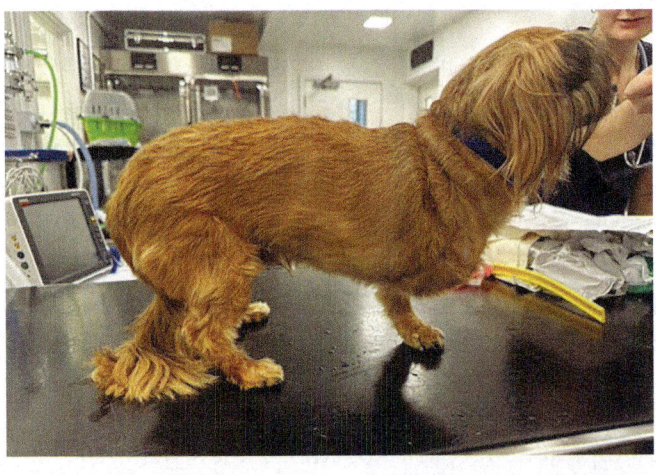

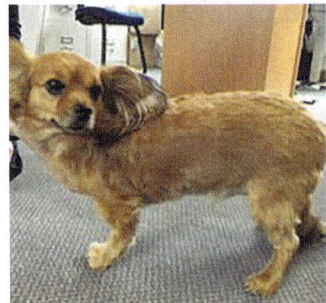
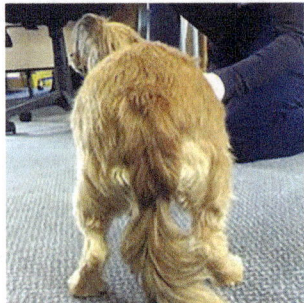

Arlo Cooperating at the Vets

I was absolutely amazed because Arlo actually cooperating was something that I definitely did not expect. I was so pleased because it made everything so much easier.

However, thinking back, I often wonder if Arlo was fully aware that we were all trying to help him and that is why he cooperated with everyone that day.

Deep down I believe that Arlo always knew exactly why the vets were going to make a cast of his body and couldn't wait for his new leg. Although of course I didn't tell anyone.

I was even more thrilled when, a few days later, I received copies of the photographs that my vet had sent to 3Dpets, along with his plaster cast. They were fantastic.

My vet was even kind enough to pack everything up for me and send it all directly to 3DPets, which was something that I had fully expected to have to do myself.

I cannot thank them enough for everything that they have done for Arlo over the years. They are an amazing, caring team and I am so pleased to say that they are still our vets today.

For the next few weeks, I was in touch with 3DPets regularly to see how things were progressing.

As I was still fundraising, and had been throughout this whole procedure, I felt that it was important to keep everyone who had been supporting Arlo fully updated.

After all, it was through their kindness that Arlo had been able to receive the care and veterinary expertise required for him to thrive and it was thanks to their ongoing support that Arlo was going to be able to have his new prosthetic.

Fortunately, 3DPets were very accommodating and informed me regularly of their progress. It was not long before I received, not only photos of his caste arriving at their offices but more importantly, a video of Arlo's new leg. I could not have been any more thrilled because 3DPets had even written Arlo's name on the side of his prosthetic and, for me, this was the icing on the cake.

It was so exciting to see Arlo's prosthetic leg for the first time and we could not wait to see little Arlo up and running about on four legs for the first time in his life, without pain.

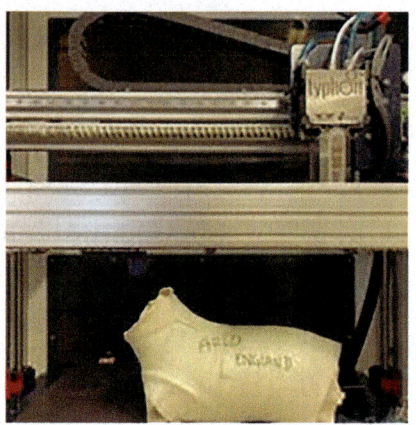

It had been an emotional journey and now that we believed that the end was in sight, it was such a relief to know that Arlo's new leg was finally on its way.

CHAPTER 23

Arlo is on Four Legs at Last

We received Arlo's leg through the post on 5th June, 2023. Fortunately, the team at 3DPets had sent the leg to me in one piece. I was so pleased because I had visions of Lyn and I trying to piece it all together.

We had chosen a bright orange for
Arlo's new prosthetic because his fur
is a beautiful rich brown colour. We
had received both the foot and the
wheel attachment for Arlo's prosthetic because 3DPets had explained
to us that the majority of smaller
dogs struggled with the foot attachment and found that the wheel was
easier to use.

If I thought that once I put Arlo's
prosthetic leg on, he would be up and running, I was very much mis-
taken. Although, once Arlo was fitted with his new prosthetic, his
alignment and body position improved beyond all recognition, Arlo
just stood there wearing his new leg paralysed with fear. Poor Arlo.

I needn't have worried because it wasn't long before Arlo began
to take his first tentative steps using his prosthetic leg, once I had
got the treats out. Although Arlo was moving and he was upright

in the perfect position, he was dragging his prosthetic instead of lifting it. When I explained this to 3DPets, they told me that this was perfectly normal and that sometimes it took dogs, especially the smaller breeds, up to a few months to be able to use their new leg confidently.

They invited me to join their group chat on Facebook and explained to me how I could contact other owners whose dogs were also just beginning their prosthetic journey.

This was a great comfort because although the majority of other owners were in the US, they all regularly posted videos of their dog's progress. I soon learned that Arlo was not the only dog to experience teething problems and it was not long before I learned how to use the wedges that I had received with the prosthetic, to get Arlo's leg into the correct position.

This was so helpful and it was not long before Arlo became more confident.

Over the weeks I took loads of photos and videos of Arlo using his prosthetic and getting around the garden with confidence and it wasn't long before Lyn and I began taking him on new adventures to places that he had never been to before.

As Arlo had been so disabled when he first arrived, he had never been able to experience the woods or the beach, without hurting his legs. He was always carried or taken there in his stroller.

I will never forget him experiencing the beach for the first time, upright and on four straight legs. To this day, I don't think that he could get over the fact that he could run with the others, and smell the rock pools and even walk on the pebbles without pain.

Another momentous moment that I will never forget is the first time that Arlo did his famous Meer cat impression, while begging for treats, with his prosthetic on. He looked so cute and adorable.

He loved the woods and over time became much more confident. He began smelling the flowers and with the leg he soon learned that having a wee was so much easier. He would stand on his prosthetic and cock his leg just like any other little dog and soon he was even joining the others and rolling in fox poo.

However, instead of being horrified like most owners, I could not have been more thrilled to see him rolling over and over and having so much fun.

Sadly, as expected by 3DPets, he did struggle using the foot attachment and it was decided that he would probably be more comfortable using the wheel.

My vet helped me to change the attachment and I must admit that although I was initially disappointed, Arlo did cope far better using the wheel.

However, the first wheel that I had received for Arlo was too large for him and after speaking to 3DPets, they agreed to make Arlo the smallest wheel that they had ever manufactured for any other dog.

What was even more exciting was that, due to its size, they decided to name this particular wheel attachment after Arlo himself.

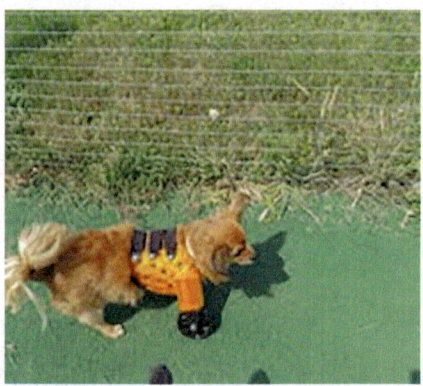

CHAPTER 24

Arlo Goes to Dog Training

I have always believed that all dogs need to go to dog training. This is because I believe that every dog needs to be stimulated, socialised and learn basic commands in a safe and secure environment.

I do not believe that a disabled dog should be treated any differently to any other dog. All of my dogs have been to dog training and have gained their preliminary certificates and I could see absolutely no reason why Arlo could not achieve the same accolades.

Do not get me wrong, I always knew that training Arlo would be a challenge, but now that Arlo was up on four legs and out of pain, I thought that dog training would be something that he would really enjoy.

Luckily, our local dog training facility, *Sussex County Dog Training*[14] were only too pleased to accept Arlo onto their books and like any other dog, give him the opportunity of gaining his certificates. Excited by the prospect of training Arlo at this fantastic facility, I booked Arlo on to the next available course

As I had explained, Arlo had been struggling using his foot attachment and we had decided that he may do better using a wheel at the end of his leg, instead of a foot. This was because Arlo had been dragging the foot along the ground, instead of picking it up.

Fortunately, his second new attachment arrived a few weeks before Arlo was due to start training. Straight away we noticed a vast improvement and although initially I had been disappointed to see Arlo using a wheel, Lyn and I had both agreed that getting Arlo the wheel attachment had been the right decision.

Arlo Goes to Training and Meets his Trainer

It wasn't long before the day arrived for me to take Arlo to his first dog training class. Although I knew of other disabled dogs, including dogs on wheels, attending dog training classes, I had never heard of any other dog wearing a prosthetic leg being trained; therefore although the prospect of training Arlo and helping him to achieve his certificates was a really exciting one, I was extremely nervous.

I kept asking myself whether or not I was doing the right thing. After all, Arlo was extremely small and had been through so much. Would he actually be able to manage a full class? Was thirty minutes of training asking too much of Arlo? I shouldn't have worried because Arlo embraced dog training, with the same bravery, tenacity and grit determination as he had everything else.

Once we got over the initial reactions of the other owners, the majority of whom were absolutely wonderful, Arlo met his dog trainer, Anna, who he instantly fell in love with.

For me, this was a bonus because Arlo did not always take to everyone, I believe that it may be because Anna was armed with treats but, in this case, I am willing to give Arlo the benefit of the doubt.

I had decided to ask my friend Lyn to come with me to dog training, not only for moral support but because I wanted her to help me carry the equipment and to take photos of Arlo's progress.

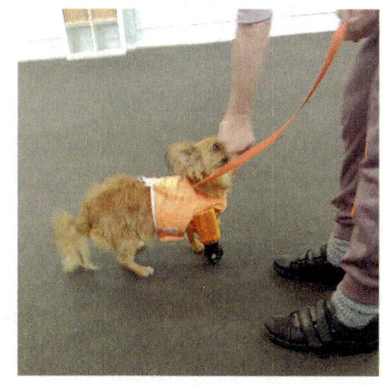

As expected, with each class came a new challenge for Arlo but he tackled each and every one head on. To be honest, Arlo even surprised me. Obviously, he did find some things more difficult than others but he appeared to really enjoy the experience.

There was only one class that Arlo absolutely hated and that was the fifth class on the course. This class was called, *'Enrichment'*, and introduced the dogs to a variety of equipment, such as boxes to stand on, tunnels to go through and other examples of the equipment the school used for agility training.

Although Arlo did try to give some of the equipment his best shot, anything that moved unexpectedly or he had to climb up onto absolutely terrified him. It was for this reason that I eventually decided to stop attending those days, until Arlo became more confident.

I could not have been more proud of Arlo, when six weeks after his first class, he was presented with his first certificate. Amazingly, despite all of the challenges that Arlo had faced during the course, he had managed to pass every single element required for his certificate, even trying a piece of equipment for the first time.

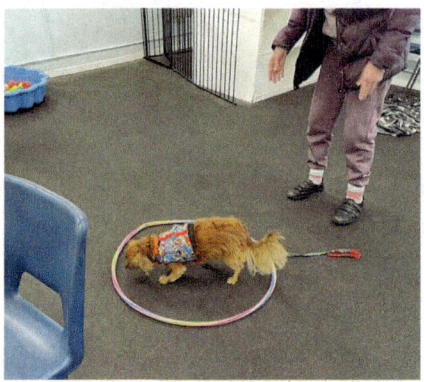

Arlo had not only achieved his Foundation certificate, which was a massive achievement for such a disabled dog, but he was now able to go up to the next grade.

CHAPTER 25

Arlo Gets a New Leg and Meets the 3DPets Team

Although Arlo had come on in leaps and bounds using his new leg, I had always felt that the leg was a tad too big and clumsy for him. Even though his stance and body position were now excellent, he looked somewhat awkward in comparison to other dogs wearing this type of prosthetic.

I knew that the only way that I could get Arlo a correctly proportioned leg was if the team from 3DPets could actually meet Arlo in person and examine him in detail. Of course, this was easier said than done because 3DPets were in the US and I absolutely hate flying.

I knew that the only way that the team and I could ever get together, was if I invited them to come to the UK, therefore that is exactly what I did.

Realistically, I knew that I needed to raise approximately £2000 for their flights and accommodation and then another £2000 for them to design and build Arlo a new leg. However, I decided that the hard work would be worth it.

I already had a little money put aside for Arlo from our previous fundraising, so I contacted Alex at 3DPets to ask him whether or not it was possible for a team member to come to the UK to examine Arlo. I also asked him, assuming a team member did come over, if they would be willing to speak to both my vet and physiotherapist.

This was because I believed that these professionals would be able to describe Arlo's disabilities, not only in more detail but technically and professionally.

Lastly and more importantly, I asked Alex whether they would be able to build Arlo a lighter smaller prosthetic.

He said that coming to the UK to help Arlo was definitely a possibility and that he would see if there was anyone from the team that was available.

Luckily, one of their leading technicians, Lydia Mindek was available and she told us that she would absolutely love to come to the UK to get to know Arlo and help him.

We arranged for her to come over to the UK in March 2024, which was just over three months away. So, once again, Lyn and I started a fundraising campaign to fund her trip.

As it was Christmastime, we decided once again to build a Christmas hamper. However, because we did not have anything to put into the hamper, we decided to ask Arlo's followers on social media to help us by donating a range of Christmas goodies to put inside.

Once again, we were flooded with gifts of everything from Christmas crackers, pudding and cake to chocolate gifts, mince pies and novelties for the children.

We were absolutely blown away by everyone's kindness and generosity. If it wasn't for all the kind people who have over the years supported and donated to Arlo's fund, none of this would have been possible and I cannot thank them all enough for their generosity.

Lyn and I were both really excited when out of the blue, we were invited to host a stall at a Christmas fair being held at one of the area's leading hotels.

We decided that we would sell a range of homemade items at the fair, including homemade dog biscuits, jams and dog toys.

Julie, a good friend and supporter of Arlo, offered to make some more jams with fruit from her allotment and Lyn and I decided that we would make some dog biscuits and dog toys.

The idea was actually better than the items that we produced and despite us both spending all day cooking and making the dog biscuits, the biscuits, even though they were made from 100% natural produce, did not look at all appetising.

I decided to try them on my dogs, to see if they were even edible, before packaging them up into individual fancy doggy themed Christmas bags.

Surprisingly, my dogs could not get enough of them, although to be fair, my dogs will eat anything if I tell them that it is a treat.

We were also lucky enough to have a beautiful range of hand knitted baby clothes, donated by an elderly lady who lived locally, for us to sell at the fair.

They were absolutely beautiful and really helped to boost our sales.

The fair was a huge success. What was even more special was the fact that the local garages had decided to donate all their tips to

Arlo, which they had been saving up in little jars with Arlo's name on.

Their gesture was so kind and it is something that I will never forget.

Slowly but surely the money came flooding in and with online auctions, generous donations and a GoFundMe page, Lyn and I eventually managed to raise all the finances required.

Arlo Meets Lydia from 3DPets

It was arranged for Lydia to fly over to the UK on 12th March, 2024. We had booked her and her mother, who had accompanied her, into a local bed and breakfast.

We decided to meet both Lydia and her mother at my vets. Luckily, Matt Gittings, who was the owner of Arun veterinary group, and who had taken over Arlo's case after my original vet had left, had agreed to meet with us all to discuss Arlo, along with physiotherapist Becky Rawlingson.

Once again, our really good friend, Derek, who ran the local pet ambulance service, agreed to drive us to the vets to meet up with everyone, as he had known little Arlo from the day that we had picked him up

Matt Gittings

I do not think that Lyn and I had ever been so nervous because meeting up with the team and introducing them to Arlo, was something that we never thought would be possible.

As Lydia and her mum walked through the door of the vets that evening, it was Arlo himself that decided to say hello to them first. He suddenly ran across the floor at a massive speed to introduce himself.

Lydia just scooped him up in her arms and gave him a cuddle saying, 'So you must be Arlo'.

After we had all introduced ourselves, Mr. Gittings, or Matt, as he prefers to be called, took us through to the physiotherapy suite so that Lydia could assess Arlo and discuss his case.

While Lydia, Matt and Becky were discussing Arlo in detail, Arlo was allowed to roam around the room doing his own thing.

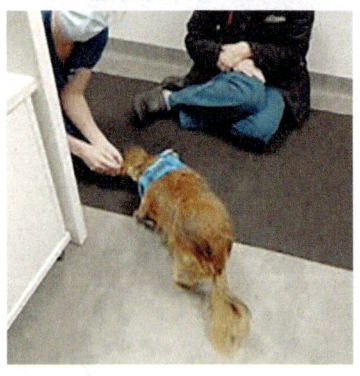

We all agreed that Arlo definitely needed a smaller, lighter prosthetic to enable him to improve and reach his full potential. Both Matt and Lydia agreed that Arlo was doing extremely well but because he was suffering from two luxating patellas, or unstable knee caps, like myself, they believed that Arlo's current prosthetic was definitely too heavy for him and that a lighter leg would really benefit him.

After the meeting, which lasted around an hour, it was decided that they should follow Derek back to their hotel.

Once Lyn and I had dropped Arlo back home, we met Lydia and her mother at the hotel for dinner.

We then arranged to meet up the next day, so that Lydia could examine Arlo and scan his body with a 3D scanner, in preparation for his new leg.

Amazingly, unbeknown to us, Lydia had arranged for us to meet up with a few other families who also had dogs using their prosthetics.

This was extremely exciting because we had never met anyone else with a dog also using one of their prosthetics and they had invited Becky along to the meeting as well.

The whole meeting was a massive success and Becky was so impressed with everything that she had seen, she decided that she would like to train with 3DPets so that she could assist them with helping other UK families.

We could not believe that Becky shared our enthusiasm and wanted to recommend 3DPets to other families and I was very keen to assist her in any way that I could.

From my own experience, Arlo's prosthetic had completely changed his life. Although he needed a lighter leg due to his size, his prosthetic had enabled him to run, jump, beg and play, just like any other little dog.

For us, helping Arlo to enrich his life and meeting up with Lydia, has been nothing short of a miracle and although Lydia was only able to stay in the UK for a few days, the whole experience is something that will remain with me forever.

While Lydia was here, she showed me just how much Arlo had impacted their lives at 3DPets.

The team had photographs of Arlo all over their walls and it was absolutely amazing for me to see them and realise just how invested in Arlo the team at 3DPets really were.

CHAPTER 26

Arlo's New Leg Arrives and Arlo is a New Dog

Once again, 3DPets were amazing and sent me regular updates on how the manufacturing of Arlo's new leg was progressing. Six weeks later, I received an update from Alex telling me that not only had they made a smaller, lighter leg for Arlo but also a two wheel cart that he could use should his legs deteriorate in the future.

I cannot thank 3DPets enough for all that they have done for Arlo. Their kindness and love for animals in distress is second to none.

The photos of Arlo's new and much improved leg were absolutely amazing and his new leg looked just perfect. The addition of the cart was especially exciting because it gave me the reassurance that should Arlo begin to struggle using his prosthetic in the future, he would have a cart that was not only designed specifically to suit his disabilities but also adapted to fit his unique size and shape perfectly.

Arlo received his new leg at the end of April 2024 and it was just perfect. I had asked 3DPets to make the harness that Arlo sits in lime green but as they were trying out tri coloured harnesses that month, I had asked them to also add in orange and blue to his harness. The results were fantastic and as the shaft of his new leg was so much smaller than his first leg, I had asked them if I could try the foot attachment again instead of the wheel.

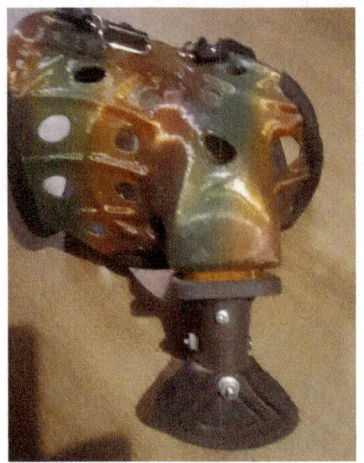

Arlo was thrilled to try on his new leg and as you can see from the photos he could not have been happier.

We believe that Arlo's new leg has made a real difference. Arlo now chases his siblings with ease. He has gone back to wearing the foot attachment because he can now lift the foot off the ground, instead of dragging it.

As we still believed that the leg section of Arlo's prosthetic was a little too long, I asked a friend of ours, Barry who runs the *Silver Wheelchair Taxies*, if he could help to shorten it. He was only too happy to help us and after a lot of trial and error and several tweaks to the leg, Barry was eventually able to get Arlo's leg the perfect length for Arlo.

As soon as he put the correctly sized leg on, Arlo was bombing around all over the place, and has not looked back since.

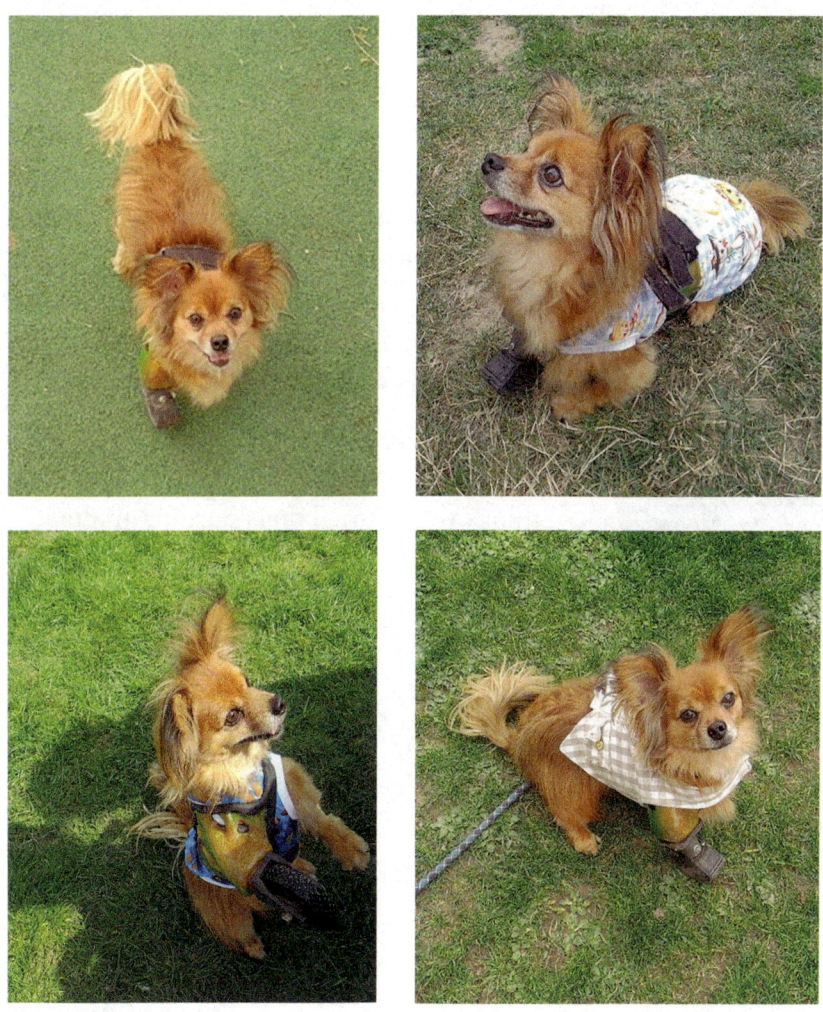

Shortly, after his new leg had arrived, Arlo went back to dog training classes and passed another two certificates. He was so confident using his new prosthetic that he even willingly participated in the enrichment class.

This was an amazing achievement for such a disabled little dog, who was rescued from certain death on a railway in Romania all those months ago.

Thanks to my vets, who believed in Arlo from day one, all the supporters who have donated over the years to help Arlo to stand tall, the two amazing surgeons who helped to fix Arlo's twisted little legs and help him be the dog that he is today, 3DPets who helped build Arlo his amazing prosthetic and all of my amazing friends, Arlo is now a confident, cheeky, happy little dog, who enjoys his walks and gets so much joy doing all of the simple things that normal dogs take for granted.

Obviously, I cannot thank everyone who has donated to Arlo's fund and supported him

from day one because the list of supporters would be endless, however, I believe that they all know who they are.

Thank you all, so much. Each and every one of you has changed Arlo's life beyond anything that I could have dreamed of. I know with certainty that if Arlo could thank you himself, he would.

It is because of you that Arlo is able to walk tall and enjoy life.

I would like to say a special thank you to Lyn, Jane and Helen for believing in me, and little Arlo, and to darling Hessa, who trusted me to care for and eventually adopt this wonderful little dog.

I would also like to thank all the amazing staff at Anderson Moores, especially the two talented surgeons who worked their magic and helped my little Arlo to hold his head up high and walk tall.

Thank you ALL so much.

If anyone reading this book is thinking about adopting a disabled dog, I would just like to say that for me it has been one of the best things that I have ever done. It has not been easy and it is not for everyone but if you think it is something that you would like to do, then it's something that I would highly recommend.

Many groups and fundraising sites have helped me to raise money for Arlo. However, as there are too many to mention individually, I am going to send out one big **THANK YOU** to you all. You all know who you are.

THE END

My Other Rescue Dogs

In total, I have seven rescue dogs and one little dog who I share the care of. All my dogs have been rescued from abroad and each of them has been rescued from a life of abuse and torture.

Five of them have disabilities and require regular medication and therapy and two of them are on special diets for life.

All of the dogs have been rescued from either the streets, kill shelters, or from illegal puppy farms.

I not only adopt injured, abused and sick dogs, I also foster and support rescues from around the world.

I am not a rescue, I do this alone and all their care, including surgery, medication, diets and therapy, is paid for out of my own pocket and through fundraising events.

If after reading this book you feel that you would like to donate towards their care, then please reach out by contacting my Facebook page Christina England *https://www.facebook.com/profile.php?id=61557805213010*

My Dogs

Meisha

Reily

Shelby

Scottie

Patsy Lou

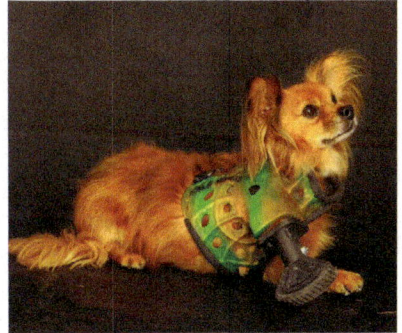

Arlo

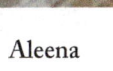

Aleena

Shared Care
Bodicia

Christina England BA (Hons)
Research Journalist and Author Bio

Christina was born and educated in London, U.K. After taking an A Level in Psychology and a BTEC in Learning Support, Ms. England spent many years researching vaccines and adverse reactions. She gained a Higher National Diploma in Journalism and Media Studies in 2010 and in 2016 she gained a BA Hons degree in Literature and Humanities. She has written on immunisation safety and efficacy for VacTruth, Health Impact News, GreenMedInfo, Vaccine Impact, Medical Kidnap and The Truth about Cancer, and is currently writing for The Liberty Beacon Project.

She has co-authored two books: Shaken Baby Syndrome or Vaccine Induced Encephalitis – Are Parents Being Falsely Accused? with Dr. Harold Buttram and Vaccination Policy and the UK Government: The Untold Truth with Lucija Tomljenovic PhD. In 2018, Ms. England compiled the book Shattered Dreams: The HPV Vaccine Exposed. All are available on Amazon.

Her website is *Parents and Carers Against Medical Injustice.*

References

1   Hessa's Homeless Hounds, Non Profit Dog Rescue in Hertfordshire –
    https://www.facebook.com/HessasHomelessHounds/?locale=en_GB

2   Babycenter – Arlo the name meaning and origin – *https://www.babycenter.
    com/baby-names/details/arlo-374*

3   Defra Guidelines - Gov UK - Bringing your pet dog, cat or ferret to Great
    Britain - *https://www.gov.uk/bring-pet-to-great-britain*

4   My social media page - Facebook – Arlo's New Beginning – *https://www.
    facebook.com/people/Arlos-New-Beginning/100064935572310/* and my new
    page Arlo's New Beginning #2
    https://www.facebook.com/profile.php?id=61559012940943#

5   Arun Veterinary Group Storrington – *https://arunvetgroup.co.uk/*

6   Montezuma's Luxury Chocolate Gifts – *https://www.montezumas.co.uk/*

7   Chihuahua Support All Paws – Facebook *https://www.facebook.com/
    groups/661909934513615/*

8   Paws and Claws Photography – Facebook group
    https://pawsandclawsphotography.co.uk/

9   Anderson Moores Veterinary Specialists – *https://www.andersonmoores.
    com/?gad_source=1&gclid=EAIaIQobChMI64zvlqS1iAMV9JFQBh3-
    UgK1EAAYASAAEgKu0PD_BwE*

10 121 Animal Therapy – *https://www.121animaltherapy.co.uk/*

11 Non-Union Fractures – Top Doctors *https://www.topdoctors.co.uk/
    medical-dictionary/non-union-fracture/https://www.topdoctors.co.uk/medical-
    dictionary/non-union-fracture/*

12 Phantom Limb Syndrome – Britannica - *Phantom limb syndrome | Causes,
    Treatment & Symptoms | Britannica*

13 3D Pets Prosthetics – *https://www.3dpetsprosthetics.com/*

14 Sussex County Dog Training *https://www.sussexcountydogtraining.com/*

Printed in Dunstable, United Kingdom

73982249R00090